A TIME TO HEAL
Healing Concepts and Testimonies

Judy Parrott
Heavens Hands Publications©

There are thousands of opinions in the world about healing, and many are strange and unusual. But only a couple views actually result in a recovery from what ails you. Examine what various people have taught about the subject and pick the one that suits you, I hope it bring the results you are hoping for!

Table of Contents

Introduction from my Heart

I love writing and sharing good news, but my goal is deeper than that. My sister and my brother are both in a battle for their lives. I was raised with their same principles of faith, but I moved to Georgia from Michigan forty years ago. My sister was eighteen. My experiences from that time are quite foreign to them.

I began visiting churches near my new home and landed in an inter-denominational one. Actually, I sensed God bringing my attention to a vacant lot near home and saying, "This is where you are going to church."

Now the church I was raised in never taught me that God talks to you, so that was new, but it was very clear in my head, and it was not my thought.

The next week, a sign appeared on the lot. "Home of Landmark Church." Okay! Confirmation that I was not hallucinating. Within a year it was my home and it still is. The sermons I heard there were rather different than I was used to. One time we were taught that you are saved purely by grace, God's favor, and your faith. I had been told I was a covenant child, chosen by

God. I didn't even accept Christ until I was 32. I didn't realize I had to make my own decision.

I almost walked out. That was far too good to be correct! Well, I stayed. The next shock was something about healing. A person came forward to share a wonderful miracle she had received from prayer. I had been convinced that miracles are in the Bible but they no longer occur today.

The one that nearly got me lost as a goose was a discussion about supernatural gifts from the Holy Spirit. (I had asked my former pastor in Michigan about it and he said God no longer offers them.)

While in my new church, my son was in deep trouble over a drug problem. I needed the support of these faithful folks, so I stayed. For years they stood in prayer and faith with me as he went through the stages addicts go through, with jail time, rehab, and finally freedom! I saw the Holy Spirit in action, setting him free, healing my husband of serious disorders from time to time, and I even learned about evil spirits and how to overcome them. I never heard any of that in my Michigan church. We had learned to be moral and we knew the Bible stories, but I for one never learned how to evangelize or set a captive free or heal anyone using Jesus' name as my authority. I learned it at Landmark. I will forever be grateful! My sister and brother are confused that my belief in such things is so strong, and frankly, they are offended at me when I share. I do not blame them a bit. I understand because I was there myself. I am writing in hopes of helping others to come to a deeper more exciting supernatural walk with Jesus. I know my family is saved and going to heaven. I just hope they won't go any time soon.

If you have been raised with a different slant on the Bible, I hope you will at least keep an open mind and then decide yourself what makes the most sense. Thank you for letting me bare my soul to you. No two people believe everything the same way. We are all exposed to different things, but we need to be tolerant and give each other space, and allow each other to communicate why we believe as we do. If it is wrong, and we are seeking what is right, we can come together lovingly. It is time for the body of Christ to unite and to heal!

Today is Friday
By Jennifer Stewart

Before I was attacked with a mysterious disease I was an aerobics instructor in my thirties, strong and a picture of health. In March 2009 I experienced a complete healing from a four-year battle with an autoimmune disease called Sjogren's Syndrome.

The type of Sjogrens I had was serious and rare and attacked my central and peripheral nervous systems leaving me in a mostly debilitated state. I was not able to work or participate in many everyday activities and was often so sick I could not live on my own or care for myself.

Aggressive medical therapies did not produce sufficient improvement. Though I had much faith and believed God for the healing manifestation, I was not seeing results. I confessed the promises of God and thought I believed them with a whole heart, but God said in **James 1:6-8 (KJV)** But let him ask in faith, nothing wavering. For he that wavereth is like a wave of the sea driven with the wind and tossed. [7] For let not that man think that he shall receive any thing of the Lord. [8] A double minded man *is* unstable in all his ways.

During my illness I had the opportunity to sit under the Word of God being taught, and while in this place of teaching, my mind was literally transformed. My mind became renewed, and I understood the truth that I was healed simply because He said I was healed, and for no other reason. His Word alone became sufficient for me, and as I quit looking to my body as an indicator of my healing, then the Truth became reality.

I finally understood that I could NOT have Sjogrens because Jesus carried it away on His back two thousand years ago and eliminated the option for it to legally be on me, according to *Matthew 8:17. I settled it in my mind that I was healed simply because He said I was, even if the symptoms never went away. I was still healed because God cannot lie.

That is when I was set free from the disease. His word became engrafted in me, and the Word became who I was. I saw myself the way Jesus sees me, and He said I wasn't sick or tired and I didn't have an autoimmune disease. He said I can run and not be weary, and I can walk and not faint.

A friend asked me a question. "Today is Wednesday. You know it is Wednesday, the scientists tell us it is Wednesday, everyone knows for certain it is Wednesday, no matter what. Your doctor agrees it is Wednesday.

If Jesus walks into your room and tells you it is Friday, what day is it?

Within three days, yes, three days, I was running three miles a day, and able to drive long distances again. My strength has been restored by the word of God and I am able to function as normal. The old has literally passed away and I am a new person. Jesus said it, therefore it is…and so I became.

My testimony is based on **Psalm 107:20 (KJV)** *He sent his word, and healed them, and delivered them from their destructions.*

I understood Jesus IS the Truth - He cannot lie. He sent His Word to me, healed me and delivered me from all destruction. Now I am a walking testimony to the goodness of God.

So what day is it? If the whole world agrees it is Wednesday, but Jesus, Lord of all the earth, creator of everything, says it is Friday? It is FRIDAY! I caught it! I hope everyone can catch it. "You will know the Truth and the Truth shall set you free."

John 1 (KJV) *In the beginning was the Word, and the Word was with God, and the Word was God.*[10] *He was in the world, and the world was made by him, and the world knew him not.*[14] *And the Word was made flesh, and dwelt among us,* **Matthew 8:17 (KJV)** *That it might be fulfilled which was spoken by Esaias (Isaiah) the prophet, saying, "Himself took our infirmities, and bare our sicknesses."*

James 5:13-20 (KJV) *[13] Is any among you afflicted? Let him pray. Is any merry? Let him sing psalms. [14] Is any sick among you? Let him call for the elders of the church; and let them pray over him, anointing him with oil in the name of the Lord: [15] And the prayer of faith shall save the sick, and the Lord shall raise him up; and if he have committed sins, they shall be forgiven him. [16] Confess your faults one to another, and pray one for another, that ye may be healed. The effectual fervent prayer of a righteous man availeth much.*

Natural versus Supernatural

Emmet Fox has a great little book called, "The Sermon on the Mount." In it he explains how the church has been misled in many ways. We have sought a purely intellectual explanation of life that is inadequate. We have built up absurd fables about a limited and man-like God who conducted his universe. Human weaknesses were attributed to Him. (This is the One who made the planets!) Legends began about original sin, blood atonements, punishment, and a doctrine of predestination to either torment or bliss! God decided who would go to heaven or to hell. We had nothing to do with it. This is not taught in the Bible. He said He would that all be saved and none be lost.

Some even say, "This or that ought to have been in the Bible." If God had not been able to protect His Bible from error he could not be God. Yes, there are versions out there that have been altered a great deal, but the trusted ones are perfect enough to guide us through life safely.

The experience of being saturated, filled to

overflowing with the Spirit of God has been reduced to something less than God intended. Some believe that when a person invites Christ into his heart, this 'baptism in the Holy Spirit' occurs at that moment. Jesus said to ask for the Holy Spirit. They have determined receiving a supernatural prayer language no longer occurs since the last apostle died because it is not mentioned after this point. So it is "no longer the evidence of this baptism." You decide.

Many have decided that the miracles Jesus and others did were greatly exaggerated by the writers of the New Testament, even though the Bible says it was all written by the inspiration of God. Some, however, believe Jesus did walk on the water but it was because it was so salty He could not sink! Well, the Sea of Galilee was fresh water. So much for that.

Why do we use our little human logic and "wisdom" to discount the wonderful things God has offered us? The real reason is that our enemy Satan offers us the tree of knowledge of good and evil to eat from. Why would he do that? This baptism Jesus offers every believer fills us with power over this enemy and his demons! It also empowers us to overcome the diseases he attacks us with! This language is essential for the spirit inside us to speak to the Father in heaven about issues we cannot even verbalize, but are important for our peace of mind. There are many more purposes for this gift we will go into later. The power of being saturated with the Spirit of God is to overcome the world, the flesh and the devil, our three enemies! Study the Book of Acts. Be armed with Truth.

Jesus, even though He was God and man, did not do any miracles until He too was baptized with the Holy Spirit. Yes, it occurred at His water baptism when the Holy Ghost came from heaven like a dove, filling Him with power to fast forty days and conquer the devil to some extent even then. He also conquered the flesh by fasting so long. He conquered the world as He rose from the dead.

Jesus is our example to follow. We are to walk and live as He did. We cannot possibly do that without the power of the Holy Spirit in us. All we need to do is ask Jesus to baptize us and He will. Many have asked, and if they "felt" nothing, they decided He had not done it. That is not the sign He said to watch for. The sign was the ability to speak with other tongues. If some would be patient and wait without doubting Him, they would receive, as they yielded their tongues to the Spirit. It may take a while for some, but God cannot lie. Don't decide it is not true just because you failed to receive...yet.

Other signs of the infilling begin to manifest in those that asked. Jesus said if we ask for His Spirit He will not give us a stone or a scorpion. He is not a deceiver. Of course we must be Christians and should be baptized before we ask. Jesus was.

Now that we are filled with His power, what do we do with it? It is given for many reasons, but mostly for service to the Body of Christ. We will each manifest different gifts that develop from His Spirit in us. One is a gift of healing. The following articles help us to help others in this gifting. Read Mark 16 and I Corinthians 12-14. This book is meant to guide us to believe for and receive healing of any sort.

Effective Prayer for Healing

Prayer is being vulnerable to and open with God, entering the Holy of Holies, because Jesus tore down the veil that once separated us from the Father. We come to Him in Jesus' name, because His payment of our sins gave us the right to become God's children.

We need to come free from unforgiveness against anyone, since Jesus forgave all our sins. We repent, or turn away from all known sin. It has been forgiven, but that does not mean we continue in it once we are aware of and have power over sin.

God said, "My people perish for lack of knowledge." It helps us to know what God promised about healing. Faith is required for answered prayers, and it comes from the Word of God, hearing it over and over. Search for His promises in the Bible.

We can obey James 5:14 and call the elders with faith to anoint us with oil. The prayer of the righteous helps our faith. Attending healing ministry meetings is a great faith-builder.

Expect God to answer. Trust Him before you see changes and continue thanking Him for what He is about to do. Rejoice while waiting. Do not turn away in doubt. If there is yet no change, examine your life if change is needed from you. A delay, however, is not God's denial. He will never leave nor forsake you.

A sample prayer for healing may go like this. Dear Father, I come in Jesus' name, depending on His blood and not my righteousness. I ask you to heal me of _____because of your promise to meet all my needs through Christ and His riches in glory. You are my Great Physician and promised to heal all my diseases. I boldly claim healing because of the stripes Jesus took for me and His shed blood that bought my salvation, my wholeness. I give you praise and joyfully expect divine health, because of your promises. Thank you for healing me, In Jesus name, Amen.

**Jesus' broken body bought our health.
His blood bought our souls.**

F.F. Bosworth wrote a wonderful book on healing. We have been so duped by seminaries that teach wrong doctrine and try to "interpret" scripture and teach it to students! It is all wrong. We must stop changing what God said!

I am seeing that the seed spoken of in the Word is not giving money to get a prayer answered. It is the Word of God sown in the heart. Plant the Word, the right seed for the situation, and eventually you will reap a crop, using God's promises as seed. Yes, as we give, we do receive, but using the word seed is not in the Bible to receive healing.

If the devil gets us to believe God won't heal us unless we stop some habit and then convinces us we can't, he has us locked right up. You can't get from God with doubts and this creates huge ones. He would love for us to quit a habit, but His love is unconditional. What should we do?

The truth is that Jesus died on the cross for two main reasons, one to save our souls and the other to give us divine health and heal our bodies. It is so clear! He wants all to be saved and all to be healed. I Tim 2:4; 2 Peter 3:9; Ezekiel 18:23. If we do not believe that we cannot get either one.

We all have vices and they are all different, but Jesus has forgiven them all, and is working on all of us to bring us closer to being like Him. We never will be this side of heaven, but as we learn about His love and acceptance of us…unconditional love…we want to please Him more all the time. It is just like our little children. They don't please us out of fear but out of a response to our love.

Why do we believe God heard our prayers? It is not a feeling. It is because He said He would. He cannot lie. He said if we know He heard us, we know we have our petition. If we doubt it, we are sort of calling Him a liar!

Some scriptures for studying this are:
Heb.6:11, 12; 10:35-36; Jonah 2:9; Heb.
13:15; Mark 11:23-24; Psalm 91:16.

Jesus healed with crowds around, and we
see the most miracles in large groups as
well, because faith is contagious. Prove.
4:20-22 says to keep the word in the midst
of your heart. It is spirit and life. Never dig
up the seed. Maintain it, water it. Be
attentive, steadfast, and enshrine the word in
your heart. Never put your eyes or mind on
symptoms. It is the wrong seed and will
produce a crop you do not want to harvest!

We need to teach healing even to the healthy
so they can pass it on and also pray for the
sick. Then they are prepared and armed if
they get attacked themselves.

Disease entered the world by sin. Romans
5:12. Doctors can assist God. They can
remove the bad stuff so God's naturally
built-in power can do the healing. See
Acts10:38 and James 5. We must be in the
habit of confessing our faults to each other.

It protects us from pride but is also a command. If we don't it may interfere with healing. Some say disease is a physical penalty of iniquity and often it is. But Jesus redeems us from iniquity and from sickness.

Some teach healing is not included in the atonement. Look up this word. I Cor 11:30 tells reasons some are sick. See 2 Cor 4:11; Lev. 14:16. Atonement healed in the OT as well.

In this world, healing is as important as salvation. Both are provided. Crucial truth. Without the shedding of blood there is no remission for sins. So Jesus is necessary for both. Salvation is based on this sacrifice. We need the whole counsel of God. He took our infirmities and bore our sicknesses. Where? On the cross and while taking the beating. (There are 39 major disease groups, and Jesus got 39 stripes-one short of 40 in case they counted wrong.) See Gal 3:7, 13, 16, 29; Job 33:24, 25; Psalm 103; I Cor 10:11.

Bottom line is that we have every right to expect healing when we ask Jesus and thank Him, standing on Mark 11:24 as our promise. It is our seed, and will grow as we study and become convinced it is true. One day we will reap what we have sown. It could even be today!

Evangelist Passes the Test

Having seen the Lord do wonderful miracles as a result of prayer and the laying on of hands since experiencing the Baptism with the Holy Spirit, I was amazed to come down myself with two deadly diseases, and I had to practice what I preached. It was not easy.

By the time the symptoms appeared, I found out I already had this strange disease, filaria, for two years. It came from a mosquito that had bitten me and planted its larvae in my body, which grew into inch-long hair-like worms that lived and multiplied in my lymphatic system. When I sat down on the worms it felt like I had ants in my pants. I couldn't sit still!

"Varicose veins," the doctor first diagnosed.

"I don't see them," I told him.

"You have internal ones, the worst kind. You may need surgery some day." So I prayed for recovery from varicose veins. There was no change. I had awful symptoms, but didn't realize worms were causing my suffering!

I left my home in America to preach as an evangelist in another country. While I was speaking one evening, an excruciating pain shot into my stomach like I was pierced with a sword! I asked for prayer from a group of men around me. I had swollen lumps all over my body and had to find what was wrong with me.

The foreign doctor said, "You have filaria. We can destroy the worms all at once but there are millions of them. Just the number of dead carcasses could kill you. You will have to take this powerful medicine for just three months, then let your body build strength and get cleaned out over the next three months. Then you must take it again for three more months." I followed his instructions. It was finally under control, except for one area of swelling that would not go away.

My doctor said, "That must be the incubation place. They are protected in that area where we can't reach them." He examined me and shocked me with the blunt statement, "You need surgery - tomorrow."

My- how dogmatic! A spirit-filled Christian doctor was telling me this. I talked to the Lord and He said, "Have the surgery. I am with you. Don't be afraid." So I had the surgery.

It was not filaria anymore. It was a fast growing cancer. The report came from the lab that I was full of it. The doctor recommended another surgery: 220 lymph nodes had to be removed. My body was full of cancer! Radical surgery was needed. I could see no choice.

Cut, cut, cut! My good doctor had prayed and believed God said he had to cut. The

Lord told me, however, "No further surgery." It was then that I went through a postgraduate course in healing.

Many laid hands on me in obedience to James 5:14. God said, "You must hold fast by sheer faith." Infection came. I experienced a lot of pain and all sorts of symptoms. I went through awful stuff. My mind kept claiming healing. A cancer specialist met with my other doctors and all agreed nothing would save my life but further immediate surgery, but God clearly said to me, "No surgery."

I learned that if you have this surgery, it takes up to three months to walk. From then on, your legs swell like balloons and you have no control over the swelling.

I learned to do homologia. That means speaking the same things as God. I waited for the manifestation of healing. I claimed my salvation in Jesus, and stood firmly on the promises he gave me in His Word. I confessed it day after day to win the battle raging in my mind. Three weeks later, the peace that surpasses understanding finally came into my mind. It guarded my heart and mind to win this spiritual and mental battle. I know now how hard it is to fight the good fight of faith.

On October 6, after the doctors had delayed and delayed x-raying my whole body, they finally did it. Not a trace of cancer was found. It was all gone!

About that time, I received letters from three missionaries, two from Ceylon and one from Taiwan. "The Lord appeared to me," said one. He told me He would heal you in three days."

Another wrote, "October 3, the Lord appeared to me and told me you were healed!"

I was healed exactly one month after the removal of the first tumor. I immediately went to preaching, though I was still weak. I quickly got my strength back, and am still preaching today. The Lord healed my body!

The Lord God reveals his plans in Jesus. He makes a move, and we must also make a move, sort of like a chess game. "Now it is your move," He says. "You must move by faith. Do not say, "If it is your will…" You must move by faith. Do something in response to the Word of God and claim healing. Make a definite claim for your healing. Got clouds of doubt in your mind? Get rid of them. Stake your claim. Rest on the Word of God. Faith is evidence of things unseen. You have it because you believe, not because you feel it. While waiting, praise the Lord and utter faith words. Let your mind be saturated with God's Word fully believed.

Some of you are waiting. Stand upon your claim and the Word of God. Learn to confess your faith. Renew your mind until you know you have the victory.

It is wonderful to be alive and be delivered from diseases.

Hebrews 11:1(KJV) Now faith is the substance of things hoped for, the evidence of things not seen.

WHY ARE SOME NOT HEALED?

There were two trees in the garden. One was the tree of the knowledge of good and evil. The other was the tree of life. The first involved logic and reasoning. The second is better than the first one. Why did

Adam not eat of that tree first? Our lives would not have tasted death. Then came Jesus, the second Adam, who restored eternal life for those who trust Him.

When one prays for healing and it does not manifest, logic generally kicks in. Reasoning has been our pattern of survival since the beginning of time. It is a hard habit to break. We can have a measure of faith, enough to ask for prayer, to pray ourselves, and to expect something to change in our bodies. But if we have placed a time frame on our miracle, and our limit is exceeded, our faith wavers.

When this happens, hope dies, and often fear takes over. Fear and faith are at opposite poles. One neutralizes the other, and our wheels begin to spin, like a car on ice.

Logic and faith cannot work up a miracle. Faith demands that we 'lean not to our own understanding'. Pr. 3:5. Logic cannot dissect a miracle without destroying it. Miracles cannot be explained. If they could, they would not be miracles, but scientific facts. For a thing to be a scientific fact, it has to be reconstructable. Under the same circumstances with no variables, an event must occur again to change a theory into a fact. Miracles do not fall in that category at all.

God is eager to show His mighty power and love to His children. This is obvious to everyone that studies the Bible. He made us to live forever. Only our sin nature brought about sickness and death. When we become His children, we become members of His kingdom. We are not of this world any longer. Our home is in heaven. We function under different rules than those of this world, and all sin is forgivable.

The law of gravity is superceded by the law of lift we see occur in an airplane. There is also a higher law than the laws of nature. This is the law that lifts us above the circumstances and into the supernatural, where miracles occur.

Faith is a gift from God. We can't muster it up. We can, however, build it into something stronger. The Bible has the power to build faith. As we study God's principles, we transform our minds to think differently, like God thinks. This is supernatural, and lifts us into a higher realm, where miracles can occur. Our human reasoning is left behind, and hope grows in us. Over time, hope turns into faith. When faith has risen, whatever we ask can come to pass. God said it in John 15. "If you abide in Me, and My words abide in you, you can ask what you will, and you shall have it."

This is the direction we must go if we need a miracle. In my life, I have seen a myriad of amazing things, but they have ebbed and waned depending on my search for God. He said if we seek Him with all our hearts, we will be found of Him. Intimacy with Him is crucial. The struggle to maintain faith is lifelong. If I let go, I will lose the most valuable treasure I have ever possessed, which is Jesus Christ Himself. In Him I live and move and have my being. Without Him, I am nothing.

Am I saying unbelief is the reason we are not always healed? Not at all; many people with strong faith sometimes live and die in pain. So what are some other reasons?

A famous evangelist claims some hindrances to healing are unbelief, a root of bitterness, ignorance of what God has promised, wrong teaching, and harboring secrets. (God said to confess our faults to each other that we may be healed.) The bottom line is when we conquer our doubts, tear down these strongholds in our minds, ask Jesus to manifest His healing in our bodies, and thank Him in advance, it is likely that we will experience a miracle of healing. We must not try to figure it out. Do we put a time frame on it? Sometimes God inspires us to know when it will occur, but not always. It can be a test of our endurance and trust as we wait expectantly for this part of our salvation to appear. Jesus said, by His stripes we *were* already healed (past tense). That is a puzzle for sure! He paid up front.

When a person is not healed if he is a Christian, depending on Christ alone for his salvation, he always has the privilege of appropriating health. Salvation is wholeness in every area of life.

Prov 3:5 Trust in the LORD with all your heart, and lean not on your own understanding.

Getting What You Need

Do you feel trapped? Can you see no way out of your situation? Do you have money in the bank? Do you get it out by sitting in the bank or do you have to do something to get it out? You have to sign your name and prove who you are with identification.

God has a procedure laid out in the Manual that must be followed to get what is yours. If you belong to God and you know Jesus paid for your sins, you are part of God's family and you have rights. You have been given salvation, a free gift that includes divine health, spiritual prosperity, peace, joy, deliverance and much more. You can believe it forever, but until you take a few simple steps, you won't possess what is yours. It will stay in the bank.

Joshua 18:3 (KJV) And Joshua said unto the children of Israel, How long *are* ye slack to go to possess the land, which the LORD God of your fathers hath given you?

The people of Israel had God's promise of protection as long as they obeyed Him that they could overtake the enemies in Canaan and have all the land, but they just sat there. They hated manna and the desert, but were unwilling to get up and go after it.

Were they afraid? Were they just depressed? Whatever it was, it kept them from the land of milk and honey, the Beautiful Land of Israel. How long will we put up with addictions, sickness and all the rest caused by the world, the flesh or the devil?

So what do we do? We read the Manual and follow the steps. Study whatever subject pertains to your situation, believe it, and then act on it. In John 5, Jesus found a paralyzed man, sick 38 years! He asked him if he wanted to be healed. We don't see the answer, except that He said, "Take up your bed and walk." He is still saying the same thing today.

Life does not give us what we deserve. It gives us what we command. We command it from the world, flesh and the devil using the ultimate weapon- words of power. Everything has to bow down before God's words. The Bible is called the Sword of the Spirit.

How did Jesus teach us by His example on the mountain of temptation? When Satan tempted Him, He always said, "It is written..." and the devil left him alone. Our flesh responds to those words as well, because faith comes by hearing the Word of God. With faith, all things are possible.

Second Kings 7 tells about a famine and four lepers that decided to go to the enemy's camp where supplies were plentiful and surrender to them. They got so desperate for something to change they figured even if they were killed, they would be out of their misery. There was a chance they might get some food and be allowed to live.

They were shocked to find that God had made the Syrians hear a noise of a huge army with chariots and horses and terrified, they all ran away, leaving all the stuff behind!

The lepers brought the news to the king, and as a result the entire city of people were saved from starvation. God had acted on their decision to move, and went ahead of them to save them. He will do the same for us. God honors His Word to perform it. His Word will not return empty, but will accomplish that for which it was sent.

God said to seek Him with a whole heart and we will be found of Him. We can seek Him by reading His mail to us, by talking to Him, by listening to the testimonies of others, by surrounding ourselves with His kids, and by total surrender to Him.

Gene was a professor who contracted a deadly disease so painful he had to crawl to the bathtub every morning before he could move his limbs to get dressed and make it to work. Finally after studying and searching for his healing a long time and feeling he was believing God, he suddenly got a brainstorm (that must have come from God). He said, "God, forgive me for being afraid of dying thinking you won't care for my family when I leave. I just surrender. I put them in your hands. You do whatever You want with me." God read his heart and saw his faith, and that very moment He healed him completely!

God will make a way when He sees a glimmer of faith and desire in you. Make a decision to shove forward, go to everything out there, read, pray, and expect to find a door opening for you. Then walk through it. God bless you!

Am I saying unbelief is the reason we are not always healed? Not at all; many people with strong faith sometimes live and die in pain. There is also a time to be born and a time to die. We don't necessarily have to die sick, but sometimes we just get tired and want to go home!

How can we Hold On?

Ben Rast of Contender Ministries writes:
"Imagine sitting in church on a bright, sunny

Sunday morning. The invocation was nice, the singing was particularly uplifting, and you managed to stick an extra couple of dollars into the collection plate. Your pastor steps to the pulpit, arranges his notes carefully, and takes a sip of water. He smiles warmly at the congregation, holds up his Bible, and announces, "Before we begin, I should let you know that I've found the Bible to be far too depressing and outdated. We shall no longer be using it in our services!" Your lower jaw is still in mid-drop when your pastor banks his former Bible off the wall and into the wastebasket. Frightening thought, no? Yet this event is happening in more and more churches around the world today; perhaps not with as much suddenness or casual flair, but the effect is the same."

One thing is certain. Change is inevitable. God is the only One that does not change. He is a constant in our lives, which is a great comfort. That means His Word also does not change, because God and the Word are one. The Word is Jesus. Look at John 1, where it says: *In the beginning was the Word, and the Word was with God, and the Word was God.* [3] *All things were made by him; and without him was not any thing made that was made. ⁱ⁰ He was in the world, and the world was made by him, and the world knew him not. ¹⁴ And the Word was made flesh, and dwelt among us, (and we beheld his glory, the glory as of the only begotten of the Father,) full of grace and truth.*

We have entered an era in which Satan, the traitor, is working harder than ever to destroy man's faith in God. *Woe to the inhabiters of the earth and of the sea! For the devil is come down unto you, having great wrath, because he knows that he has but a short time.* Rev. 12:12

How does this enemy work to harm us? In wartime, soldiers study their enemy's tactics to defeat them, the same way God expects us to defeat Satan. Clues abound in our manual, the Bible. No wonder Satan tries to convince mankind that God's Word cannot be trusted. Even in the Garden of Eden he destroyed Eve's faith in God. "Has God really said…?" 1 Timothy 4:1 says: *Now the Spirit speaks expressly, that in the latter times some shall depart from the faith, giving heed to seducing spirits, and doctrines of devils.* 2 Timothy 4:3 *For the time will come when they will not endure sound doctrine; but after their own lusts shall they heap to themselves teachers, having itching ears...*

Many mainstream churches now preach strange doctrines and even deny the virgin birth of Christ. Others allow perverted pastors to teach them what the Word "really" says about homosexuality and other abominations to God. Some already teach that there are many ways to heaven, to include all religions. God warned us about these times. Satan's subtle deceptions have come into the church in these last days before the return of Jesus.

The most popular movies and cartoons for children now teach witchcraft and Hindu reincarnation in such subtle forms. Mature Christians often overlook what 'eager to learn' children are absorbing as part of their belief system. *Avatar* and *Harry Potter* are such examples. It is said that the word *Avatar* means reincarnation. 2 Thessalonians 2:3 says: *Let no man deceive you by any means: for that day shall not come, except there come a falling away first, and that man of sin be revealed, the son of perdition;*

What hope do we have? Will we all fall away before Jesus comes back for us? Even Jesus said, *"Will I find faith on the earth when I return?"* How can we hold on? The manual covers it, of course. We study the Truth. We also examine Satan's tactics. 2 Corinthians 2:11 *Lest Satan should get an advantage of us: for we are not ignorant of his devices.* Buy a large concordance, like Strong's, and look up key words to study, such as 'overcome,' 'conquer,' and everything the Holy Spirit shows you. These tools equip the saints with sword scriptures for spiritual warfare.

We trust Jesus to save us and not ourselves or our good works. Jude 1:24 *Now unto him that is able to keep you from falling, and to present you faultless before the presence of his glory with exceeding joy...* Rev. 12:11 says: *And they overcame him by the blood of the Lamb, and by the word of their testimony; and they loved not their lives unto the death.*

I never considered myself a sinner until I was 32 and God showed me I was, just like everyone else in the world. That was when

James Kennedy also presented the solution. Only blood could erase my sins, according to God, and the sacrifice had to be perfect, just like God demanded in the Old Testament. Jesus offered His own blood to God, and died in my place. I finally obeyed God by inviting Christ into my life and surrendered my will to Him.

This is a wonderful promise. 2 Peter 1:10 *Wherefore the rather, brethren, give diligence to make your calling and election sure: for if ye do these things, ye shall never fall:*

We study the manual every day. Our spirit requires daily bread. Why do Christians fall away? God said, *My people perish for lack of knowledge.* If a pastor begins teaching wrong doctrines, we can discern the truth and call him on it. This is our responsibility, not to argue, but to keep him accountable. He is only human. We are to put our trust in no man, but in God alone.

God is our constant, our foundation and hope. He does not change. He is the Word. It can be trusted when everything around us falls apart. Nothing else can do what God can and wants to do for us, because He loves us unconditionally. As we transform our minds to think like He does, we will change, and become like Him. For these reasons, we will never fall away. Maranatha! Jesus, come quickly!

God created us to have fellowship with Him. When we do that, He reveals things to us and shows us what we need to understand. Simple, isn't it?

I met George at church one day before God healed him. He was terribly emaciated with huge bumps all over his face. He scared the children who saw him, but it all changed over time. I can testify he was healed, but of course you don't know me, do you? This is his story.

Healed of Aids
George M.

In 1996, I developed a cough and warts started to appear on my face. I thought this was the result of a stressful lifestyle. It continued to get worse as the months passed and I began to lose my memory.

This prompted me to visit my doctor. A few days after the visit, on April 22, 1997, I was rushed to the emergency room. The results of a spinal tap confirmed the doctor's suspicion that I had spinal meningitis. I was given heavy dosages of antibiotics following a battery of tests; then my doctor informed me I also had AIDS.

I never dreamed I would be one of those who would contract this dreaded disease. In a follow-up visit a few weeks later, the doctor told me that not only did I have the HIV infection; I was in the last stages of AIDS.

The hospital chaplain who visited me said I would have twelve to eighteen months (at most) to live. My response to her was, "Miracles do happen." She replied, "I have never seen anyone overcome AIDS. The people I have encountered are already dead." The chaplain gave me no hope but there was something deep within me that reached out to God. I knew medication would not help me at this point. I truly believed God was my only and last hope.

I was discharged from the hospital and I returned to my apartment to face hours and hours of depression and loneliness. I had plenty of time to reflect on my life. Growing up of Hispanic descent, I had been reared in the Catholic tradition along with my seven brothers and three sisters. I remember from various church sermons that if anyone was sick, they should call on the elders of the church for anointing with oil and prayer.

Not knowing where to go or what to do, I phoned a fellow Catholic friend for advice. She advised me, "Find a church that prays for the sick."

I phoned a church next door to my apartment complex, and asked, "Do you believe God can heal people with AIDS?" I felt relieved when they said yes, and I asked them to help me.

The following day, the elders came over to anoint me with oil and pray. During their visit, they encouraged me to forgive anyone who had ever hurt me. Believing the Lord had led these people into my life, I decided to follow their advice.

Hour after hour, I recalled various aspects of my dysfunctional childhood. There were so many things that happened in our home that caused anger, bitterness, resentment and hurt.

The youngest of eleven children, I had

watched my brothers and sisters do all the grocery shopping and other errands because my dad insisted my mother remain at home. Occasionally, Mom was allowed to visit her sisters who lived down the street. I will leave it at that to honor my parents.

I didn't understand Jesus Christ until I was a teenager. One of my sisters shared her knowledge of the Lord with me. When I finally understood Christ's role, I accepted Him as my Lord and Savior and I experienced the baptism of the Holy Spirit.

Unfortunately, I walked away from Him shortly after and did not commit to the life of a Christian.

It was around that time that I became attracted to other boys in my classes. In many ways, I believe I was looking for some acceptance and attention that was lacking in my relationship with my dad.

Whenever these thoughts came, I told myself this is a phase I'm going through and it will pass. My brothers are dating girls and soon I will be, too.

In the 11th grade, however, I gave in to my feelings and had my first homosexual experience. By the time I entered 12th grade, I had given myself completely to the homosexual lifestyle.

Upon realizing my hometown was too small for the gay lifestyle, I moved to another state to be with my sister who had been kicked out of the house.

For the next several years, I moved from city to city hitting all the gay bars and thoroughly enjoyed exploring all the avenues of the gay lifestyle. When I did not have a partner, I was sexually promiscuous. I never liked living or being alone. I was always on the lookout for another lover.

Eventually, I became tired of the sexual encounters. While drinking with my friends I would often ask, "Why are we here? There has to be more to life than sex and drinking." No answer satisfied me. At other times, I would ask myself, if I were to die today, would I go straight to heaven or hell? There was always a voice that would say, "You're going straight to hell," but I would continue to justify my lifestyle by saying I was basically a good person.

Through these years, I knew what I was doing was wrong. However, my need for love and acceptance was so great, it seemed impossible for me to break free.

In the ensuing days as I learned more about my deteriorating health, I fully realized my need for the Lord to intervene. In almost every church service I attended, people anointed me with oil and prayed over me.

When my doctor told me I was in the last stages of AIDS in May of 1997, I said to him, "I have accepted Jesus Christ as my Lord and Savior. God is going to heal me!"

He replied, "I don't want to get your hopes up, but I have been a doctor for many years and I haven't seen one miracle yet."

I insisted, "Well, you are going to see it, and you are going to believe it."

The doctor started me on AZT, but I knew that medications would not help me at this point. During the first week of medication, I was not getting any better. One Saturday I felt so miserable and looked so horrible, I cried out to God, "Please take me home!" I wanted to die, and knew it would be better to be with Him than to stay here weak and in pain.

Later, I heard the Lord say, "I'm not ready to take you home. I am going to heal you."

Every day I progressively got worse. On Sunday morning, June 1, 1997, I woke up feeling very ill and weak...the worst I had ever felt. I said to God that morning, "If I have to crawl to church, I will crawl. I just need to be in Your presence."

At the conclusion of the morning worship, several church members gathered around me and anointed me with oil again.

As they laid their hands on me, something different happened during this prayer session. I sensed the healing power of God throughout my body. I cried for a long time as I accepted His grace and I believed the disease had left me. Following the prayer, I literally ran back to my apartment, praising God for His love and mercy.

In a follow-up visit the next morning, my physician told me my viral load test completed the last time was extremely high and said, "It's imperative that this drops!"

Without hesitation I said, "You are going to see a big drop this time." During that month of waiting for the test results, I began to gain weight. The warts started to clear up and my energy began returning to normal.

At the next appointment, the doctor shared the results of the tests. The viral load had dropped from 102,820 down to 613! I was elated with the results but I did not need them to prove anything. Everything I was experiencing in my body had already convinced me that God had healed me!

A month later, another viral load blood test was taken. In those test results, traces of the AIDS virus could not be detected! The doctor was speechless and had no explanation. His comment months later was, "Either you are extremely lucky with this medication or this was an act of God."

As the months passed, my physical strength continued to increase and my appetite returned to normal. Now I am off all medications.

As I reflect on the last fifteen years of my life, especially the past eighteen months, I have learned so many things about who I am and who God is. I am a living testimony of the miraculous power of God. Words cannot express how grateful I am for my complete healing of this incurable disease.

Though I walked away from God during my teenage years, He did not forget me. His mercy is infinite.

I am also very grateful for the healing of my painful emotional past. When I forgave the people who hurt me, I was set free from an emotional prison.

Accepting God's forgiveness for myself was even more powerful. I am continually reminded of how much God loves us. No matter how horrible you may feel about your life choices, God is quick to forgive. Simply open your heart to Him and He will wipe your slate clean.

My faith and trust in God were tested through this experience and now I feel the incredible strength of His Spirit within me. I have come to realize that no person can ever meet the deepest emotional needs of my life. Only God can meet those needs.

I have chosen a celibate life. I continue to seek His help, guidance and wisdom. The more I know Him, the more I feel closer to Him.

God's ways cannot be explained. If you have an incurable disease or have doubts about God's power, remember me. Repent of (turn from) your sins. Forgive yourself and the people of your past. Most importantly, believe with all your heart that God can heal you. He is omnipotent and He works to accomplish His purpose in you.

James 1:15 *Then when lust hath conceived, it bringeth forth sin: and sin, when it is finished, bringeth forth death.*

Psalm 103:2-3 *Bless the LORD, O my soul, and forget not all his benefits: 3 Who forgiveth all thine iniquities; who healeth all thy diseases...*

Medical Science is now saying that people with faith recover from illness quicker than people who do not have faith.

Two Trees-One Brings Life

There were two trees in the garden. One was the tree of life and the other the tree of the knowledge of good and evil. Which one did God want Adam to eat from? Which one did he choose? What was the result?

We still eat from that tree. We depend on our own intellect, our brilliant scientists, our human logic to figure out the things of God. We make judgments based on experience rather than the Word of God which is life to our flesh and health to our bones.

Can we trust God? Do we question what we observe? Do our experiences bring us doubts? When God says He heals all our diseases, why are some not healed? Is it God who dropped the ball? Is it His plan to heal only some but not others? If so, which ones? If we have doubts about whether it includes us, does this make us double-minded? God said a double-minded person gets nothing from Him.

Jesus already paid the price for us to live healthy lives. It says by His stripes we WERE healed. Then why don't we see everyone healed?

God has the answer to all these questions, so watch carefully.

What is Cessationism?

The first time I heard the message of God's grace, His undeserved favor, I left that church, believing it was a false church! It is so foreign to many denominations that have been taught the concept of "cessationism." It is such a false belief, but somehow in these last days it has caught on in most churches.

God warned this would happen in the end times and it is.

What the enemy means for evil, God turns out for good.

We are in the end times, meaning Christ is about to return to earth and bring His followers home to heaven. He promised it to His disciples and it is still forthcoming. The prophetic signs of His return have nearly all come to pass. We will go into that later.

Jesus said in the end times there will be great deception, to the extent that if it were possible, even His chosen people would be deceived. Jesus even said, "Will I find faith on the earth when I return?" Satan goes to the top, to those who influence others, in order to deceive. He goes to the teachers.

"Cessationist" Christianity holds to the view that the supernatural gifts such as healing, speaking in tongues and prophesying were used as signs to confirm the validity of who Jesus and his followers were and that they are no longer necessary for the church.

Some also believe the position of Apostle no longer exists. Ask google the meaning of cessationism. Ask your pastor what he believes as well. It is important.

One type of church teaches the Bible rather literally. Others leave out important information about the Holy Spirit, the third part of the Trinity. It begins in the seminaries where the future pastors are being taught what to preach. It is important to know to get through this life victoriously. We need all the tools God offers.

Satan's deception to divide the church with disagreements often involves the Holy Spirit. He plants lies in our minds. One lie is that God no longer baptizes or immerses us with His Spirit. He twists the verse that says: "When the perfect comes, tongues will pass away and knowledge will pass away." Some seminaries interpret that to mean "the perfect" is the completed New Testament. "Once it was completed, there was no longer any use for other tongues, so they are no longer available." It makes no sense.

Knowledge has not yet passed away. As a matter of fact, God said in the end, knowledge would increase. We have not seen so much knowledge since the world began!

Some Christians view the miracles in the Bible as being limited to that time period when God was most forceful in proving his influence. In the Full Gospel circles, those that believe the Bible more literally, these miracles still occur and include healing and speaking in tongues.

This gift, the 'least of the spiritual gifts', but still very important, is a private language Satan cannot understand, though there are times we speak in a known language, but there are two types of tongues. One is personal. I Cor.14:2 It is a miracle to be able to open your mouth and decide not to speak English and a real language comes out. It has been proven your frontal lobe is dormant while speaking this other language! So it comes from the spirit.

It is nonsense to deny this gift exists today. Over 200 million Christians have the ability to pray this way. The most powerful ministries are those that simply accept the Bible as factual for today as well as in the days of the apostles and prophets of old.

So what do they believe, teach and manifest? They believe the book of Acts is for today. When Jesus left the earth, He said, "Go and tarry in Jerusalem, and wait for the Holy Spirit. He cannot come until I get to heaven. I will send Him to you." So 500 people who watched Jesus leave the earth in a cloud returned and waited in an upstairs hall or large room. They got a bit disillusioned, though, when it did not happen for ten more days, until the day of Pentecost, when people from all over the area were in the city to celebrate the feast.

By then, only 120 had stuck it out and remained. Suddenly the room was filled with a powerful wind-inside! Tongues of fire appeared on every head! And each one began babbling in strange languages! The spirit led them outside where foreigners heard them all speaking in their various languages, the message about Jesus! This is how the church spread around the world.

When the entire experience of this supernatural baptism is eliminated, all the gifts God has for us go in the trash as well, because it is this experience that brings in these wonderful gifts. You see miracles very rarely in those churches that do not teach that this is for today. You hardly ever hear about healings, and prophecy is not even allowed in these churches. They have also been taught that prophecy is simply preaching. It is so much more.

There are nine spiritual gifts that we can receive from the Holy Spirit. They vary with each person as God chooses to give different ones to each of us. There are gifts of healings, a gift of miracles, a gift of speaking in diverse tongues, a gift of interpreting the tongues, a gift of prophecy, a gift of supernatural knowledge, a gift of supernatural wisdom, a gift of discerning spirits, and a gift of special faith.

The dove is a symbol of the Holy Spirit. Doves have nine feathers on each side. One side symbolizes the nine gifts of the spirit. The other side signifies the nine fruits of the spirit. He has five tail feathers that stand for the fivefold leader ministry gifts: prophets, pastors, teachers, evangelists and apostles. Doves are interesting and unique. They mate for life, and tears come out of their eyes!

If you need a miracle from God, you need great faith. You need the power of the Holy Spirit to have great faith. You need to ask Jesus to baptize you (immerse you) with His Holy Spirit. Then you need to yield to Him and allow Him to come into you. If you ask, Jesus won't give you a stone or a scorpion, He said He will give you the Holy Spirit. He is already with you, and He will fill you with Himself. Then you will begin to see supernatural things happen. Healing and miracles are available to you in a deeper measure. Your ability to understand the

Bible will become deeper, greater. A whole new dimension opens up, as you will see. Yield your tongue but use your vocal cords and try to just let God use your voice. If you only get one word, speak it, and more words will gradually manifest. That is faith working.

You will desire meaty spiritual teaching, and not just milk, like babies drink. "Full gospel churches" and charismatic (means grace) churches will fulfill you in a way you may have never tasted. I hope this letter has enlightened and encouraged you! The best is yet to come!

He is "the same yesterday and today and forever" (Hebrews 13:8) and with that faith that God acts in the world today the same way as in ancient times.

The Second Blessing

Salvation is normally viewed as a long-term one-step process for Christians. In the Full Gospel Church, another level of salvation is recognized. It is called the 'second blessing' and those baptized in the Full Gospel Church make it their foremost goal.

The first blessing is secured through believing Jesus was crucified, dead, and resurrected and confessing it. Then being baptized in water is the outward sign of our belief. Reaching the second blessing is simply asking Jesus to baptize us with His Holy Spirit and trusting Him.

Spiritual healing arises from the belief in miracles. Prayer is considered an essential step in overcoming disease. Energetic services where people seemingly recover from disability or sickness immediately are flagships of Full Gospel and Pentecostal services.

There has been controversy as some churches encourage people to bypass modern medical intervention and rely solely on faith healing and prayer. It should be emphasized, though, that is not the usual belief of most Full Gospel churches. Most believe God uses doctors and knowledge as well as faith in healing.

Faith goes beyond rituals and dogma, and extends into action and full involvement in religious services. Being expressive during church is a large part of Pentecostal practices.

Guaranteed Cures for What Ails You from Jesus, who Loves you Best

The Word of God for the sick person is the GOS-Pill. Take them every day and I promise you will recover. When you mind becomes the same as God's mind pertaining to healing, you will be well.

First of all, if you have never given your life to Jesus Christ, you need to be saved. Romans 10:9 and 10 says, "If you confess with your mouth the Lord Jesus and believe in your heart that God has raised Him from the dead, you will be saved. For with the heart one believes to righteousness, and with the mouth confession is made to salvation." Give Jesus lordship of your life. Repent of your sins and confess Him as your Lord and Savior and as your Healer. Then you can have confidence to believe God for your complete healing.

God cannot lie. He is the Spirit of Truth, so He can be trusted. If He said the Bible is the Word of God, this is what it is, whether we understand how it was brought forth, or not.

His ways are above our ways, and we will never understand all about God.

My son...give attention to my words; incline your ear to my sayings. Do not let them depart from your eyes; keep them in the midst of your heart; for they are life to those who find them, and health to all their flesh. Proverbs 4:20-22

I will restore health to you, and heal you of your wounds. Jeremiah 30:17

By your words you are justified, and by your words you are condemned.

A double-minded man receives nothing from the Lord.

The Word of God will save your life.

Not a word failed of any good thing which the Lord had spoken...All came to pass. Joshua 21:45 (God's Word will not fail)

For it is God who works in you both to will and to do for His good pleasure. Philippians 2:13 (God's will- healing- is working in you.)

He who raised Christ from the dead will also give life to your mortal bodies through His Spirit who dwells in you. Romans 8:11 (the Spirit of Life is making your body alive.)

For all the promises of God in Him and Yes, and in Him, Amen, to the glory of God through us. 11 Corinthians 1:20(God is for you.)

Lord, if you are willing, you can make me clean. (the leper said to Jesus). (Jesus said...) I am. Be clean." Matthew 8: 2, 3 (It is God's will for you to be healed.)

If you diligently heed the voice of the Lord your God and do what is right in His sight, give ear to His commandments and keep all His statutes, I will put none of the diseases on you which I have brought on the Egyptians. (In the permissive sense). For I am the Lord who heals you. Exodus 15:26 (Obey God's Word and be healed. God's promises are conditional...Hebrews 11:6 says God is a rewarder of those who diligently seek Him.)

So you shall serve the Lord your God, and He will bless your bread and your water. And I will take sickness away from the midst of you." Exodus 23:25 (Serve the Lord and healing will be yours.)

And the Lord will take away from you all sickness. (Notice it doesn't say, "I will take some, but ALL) and will afflict you with none of the terrible diseases of Egypt which you have known, but will lay them on all those who hate you." Deut. 7:15

Bring all the tithes in to the storehouse, that there may be food in My house, and prove Me now in this, says the Lord of hosts, "If I will not open for you the windows of heaven and pour out for you such blessing that there will not be room enough to receive it." Malachi 3:10 (Obey all God's command-ments and receive all His blessings.)

Bless the Lord, O my soul; and all that is within me, bless His holy name! Bless the Lord, O my soul, and forget not all His benefits... Psalm 103:1-5 (One of God's benefits is healing.)

(What are His benefits?) Psalm 103:7

Who forgives all your iniquities, who heals all your diseases, who redeems your life from destruction, who crowns you with loving kindness and tender mercies, who satisfies your mouth with good things, so that your youth is renewed like the eagle's.

He sent His word and healed them, and delivered them from their destructions. Psalm 107:20.

I shall not die, but live, and declare the works of the Lord. Psalm 118:17 (God wants you to live.)

I call heaven and earth as witnesses today against you, that I have set before you life and death, blessing and cursing; therefore choose life, that both you and your descendants may live. Deut. 30:19 (Choose to live. Be a fighter!)

With long life I will satisfy him, and show him My salvation. Psalm 91:16 (You will live a long life.)

He was wounded for our transgressions, He was bruised for our iniquities; the chastisement for our peace was upon Him, and by His stripes we are healed. Isaiah 53:5 (Jesus bore your sins and your sicknesses.)

He Himself took our infirmities and bore our sicknesses. Matter 8:17

For I will restore health to you and heal you of your wounds. Jeremiah 30:17 (God will restore your health.)

Assuredly, I say to you, whatever you bind on earth will be bound in heaven, and whatever you loose on earth will be loosed in heaven. Matthew 18:18 (You can take authority over the sickness in your body.)

Again I say to you that if two of you agree on earth concerning anything that they ask, it will be done for them by My father in heaven.   Matthew 18:19 (Agree with someone for your healing.)

Have faith in God. For assuredly, I say to you, whoever says to this mountain, 'Be removed and be cast into the sea, 'and does not doubt in his heart, but believes that those things he says will come to pass, he will have whatever he says. Mark 11:22,23 (What you say will make a difference.)

Proverbs 6:2 We are snared by the words of our mouth...so be careful what comes out.

Therefore I say to you, whatever things you ask when you pray, believe that you receive them, and you will have them. Mark 11:24 (Believe, and you will receive.)

I, even I, am He who blots out your transgressions for My own sake; and I will not remember your sins. Put Me in remembrance; let us contend together; state your case, that you may be acquitted. Isaiah 43:25,26. (Plead your case to God.)

And these signs shall follow those who believe...they will lay hands on the sick, and they will recover. Mark 16:17, 18 (Have someone lay hands on you for healing.)

If anyone is a worshipper of God and does His will, He hears him, John 9:31 (Learn to Worship God- praise Him, Pray.)

The thief does not come except to steal, and to kill, and to destroy. I have come that you may have life, and that you may have it more abundantly. John 10:10 (The devil wants to kill you; God wants to heal you.)

Christ has redeemed us from the curse of the law, having become a curse for us (for it is written, Cursed is everyone who hangs on a tree), that the blessing of Abraham might come upon the Gentiles in Christ Jesus. Galatians 3:13,14. (You are redeemed from the curse.)

Let us hold fast the confession of our hope (faith), without wavering, for He who promised is faithful. Hebrews 10:23 (You will not waver in your faith.)(Other thoughts do come into our mind, but this is not a loss of faith. They come from outside of us.)

Therefore do not cast away your confidence, which has great reward. Hebrews 10:35 (You can have confidence in God and His word.)

Let the weak say, "I am strong." Joel 3:10 (You can find strength in God and in His Word.)

Let him take hold of My strength. Isaiah 27:5

Jesus Christ is the same yesterday, today, and forever. (Jesus Christ has never changed. What He did in the Bible, He will do for you today.) Hebrews 13:8

Beloved, I wish above all things that you may prosper and be in health, even as your soul prospers. 3rd John 2. (God's highest wish is for you to be well.)

Is any among you sick? Let him call for the elders of the church, and let them pray over him, anointing him with oil in the name of the Lord. And the prayer of faith will save the sick, and the Lord will raise him up. And if he has committed sins, he will be forgiven. James 5:14, 15 (Be anointed with oil by a Christian who believes in healing.)

...who Himself bore our sins in His own body on the tree, that we, having died to sins, might live for righteousness- by whose stripes you were healed. 1 Peter 2:24(Jesus has already paid the price for your healing.)

Now this is the confidence that we have in Him, that if we ask anything according to His will, He hears us. And if we know that

He hears us, whatever we ask, we know that we have the petitions that we have asked of Him. 1 John 5:14,15 (Be confident in your prayers.)

Beloved, if our heart does not condemn us, we have confidence toward God. And whatever we ask we receive from Him, because we keep His commandments and do those things that are pleasing in His sight. 1 John 3:21,22. (God answers the prayers of those who keep His commandments.)

For God has not given us a spirit of fear, but of power and of love and of a sound mind. 11 Timothy 1:7 (Fear is not of God. Rebuke it!)

For the weapons of our warfare are not carnal, but mighty through God to the pulling down of strongholds; casting down imaginations, and every high thing that exalts itself against the knowledge of God, and bringing into captivity every thought to the obedience of Christ. 11 Cor. 10:4,5. (Cast down those thoughts and imaginations that don't line up with the Word of God.)

Finally, my brethren, be strong in the Lord and in the power of His might. Put on the whole armor of God, that you may be able to stand against the wiles of the devil. For we do not wrestle against flesh and blood, but against principalities, against powers, against the rulers of darkness of this age, against spiritual hosts of wickedness in the heavenly places.

Therefore take up the whole armor of God, that you may be able to withstand in the evil day, and having done all, to stand. Ephesians 6:10-13 (Be strong in the Lord's power. Put on His armor to fight for your healing.)

Stand, therefore, having girded your waist with truth, having put on the breastplate of the preparation of the gospel of peace; above all, taking the shield of faith with which you will be able to quench all the fiery darts of the wicked one. And take the helmet of salvation, and the sword of the Spirit, which is the word of God. Ephesians 6:14-17

And they overcame him by the blood of the Lamb and by the word of their testimony, (and loved not their lives unto death.)(This goes with ...he who saves his life will lose it, but he who loses his life for my sake shall save it.) Revelation 12:11 (Give testimony of your healing.)

Affliction will not rise up a second time. Nahum 1:9 (Your sickness will leave and not come back again.)

Is Cessationism biblical? What is a Cessationist?

Cessationism is the view that the "miracle gifts" of tongues and healing have ceased; that the end of the apostolic age brought about a cessation of the miracles associated with that age. Most cessationists believe that, while God can and still does perform miracles today, the Holy Spirit no longer uses individuals to perform miraculous signs.

The biblical record shows that miracles occurred during particular periods for the specific purpose of authenticating a new message from God. Moses was enabled to perform miracles to authenticate his ministry before Pharaoh (Exodus 4:1-8). Elijah was given miracles to authenticate his ministry before Ahab (1 Kings 17:1; 18:24). The apostles were given miracles to authenticate their ministry before Israel (Acts 4:10, 16). Jesus' ministry was also marked by miracles, which the Apostle John calls "signs" (John 2:11). John's point is that the miracles were simply proofs of the authenticity of Jesus' message.

After Jesus' resurrection, as the Church was being established and the New Testament was being written, the apostles demonstrated "signs" such as tongues and the power to heal. "Tongues are for a sign, not to them that believe, but to them that believe not" (1 Corinthians 14:22, a verse that some claim plainly says the gift was never intended to edify the church.

1 Cor 14:4 says tongues edifies and improves a person. 1 Cor 12:7-11 tells the manifestation of the Spirit is given for the common good.

This is taught in many churches, not always directly:

The Apostle Paul predicted that the gift of tongues would cease (1 Corinthians 13:8). Here are six proofs in their opinion that it has already ceased:

1) The apostles, through whom tongues came, were unique in the history of the church. Once their ministry was accomplished, the need for authenticating signs ceased to exist.

2) The miracle (or sign) gifts are only mentioned in the earliest epistles, such as 1 Corinthians. Later books, such as Ephesians and Romans, contain detailed passages on the gifts of the Spirit, but the miracle gifts are not mentioned, although Romans does mention the gift of prophecy. The Greek word translated "prophecy" means "speaking forth" and does not necessarily include prediction of the future. It likely simply means preaching.

3) The gift of tongues was a sign to unbelieving Israel that God's salvation was now available to other nations. See 1 Corinthians 14:21-22 and Isaiah 28:11-12.

4) Tongues was an inferior gift to prophecy (which they define as simply preaching).

Preaching the Word of God edifies believers, whereas tongues does not. Believers are told to seek prophesying over speaking in tongues (1 Corinthians 14:1-3).

My notes: Prophecying means more than simply preaching. Look it up. It sometimes foretells the future. Yes, Satan counterfeits all the gifts, including this one. But Jesus said if we ask for the Spirit He will not give us a scorpion! Not to worry. And Satan cannot counterfeit love and the fruits of the Spirit.

There are two types of tongues. One is a language that requires interpretation in a church setting, not the personal private tongue which evidences the receiving of the Holy Spirit by HS baptism. They are two different things entirely, with different functions. The private tongue is for prayer and intercession. The public one is for use in the church for the building up and edifying of the body of Christ. Not all have this gift.

The cessation theory also teaches:

5) History indicates, they say, that tongues ceased. Tongues are not mentioned at all by

the Post-Apostolic Fathers. Other writers such as Justin Martyr, Origen, Chrysostom, and Augustine decided that tongues happened only in the earliest days of the Church.

My notes: The possibility they did not believe in the Baptism of the HS was not proof it does not exist today. All evidence shows the opposite. Joel 2 speaks of things happening more in the last days. Here we are!

6) They believe current observation confirms that the miracle of tongues has ceased. If the gift were still available today, they reasoned, there would be no need for missionaries to attend language school. (*Typical human logic.*) Missionaries would be able to travel to any country and speak any language fluently, just as the apostles were able to speak in Acts 2. As for the miracle gift of healing, we see in Scripture that healing was associated with the ministry of Jesus and the apostles (Luke 9:1-2). And we see that as the era of the apostles drew to a close, healing, like tongues, became less frequent. (*My note: this is pure conjecture!*) The Apostle Paul, who raised Eutychus from

the dead (Acts 20:9-12), did not heal Epaphroditus (Philippians 2:25-27), Trophimus (2 Timothy 4:20), Timothy (1 Timothy 5:23), or even himself (2 Corinthians 12:7-9). The reasons for Paul's "failures to heal" are 1) the gift was never intended to make every Christian well, but to authenticate apostleship; and 2) the authority of the apostles had been sufficiently proved, making further miracles unnecessary. (*My note: I can see this person is not one in a wheelchair or dying of some Satanic deadly disease!* We need miracles today as well!)

(My notes; This is natural human reasoning, not supernatural revelation by any means! Current observation depends on where you are observing! To call over 200 million tongue-speaking Christians unbiblical (or even accusing them of serving Satan!) is like putting one's head in the sand like an ostrich. Google says there are over 279 million Pentecostals in the world.)

My Miracle

Dr. Collins has declared that I have NO spinal curvature as my former ex-rays have shown! God healed me! JP

Proverbs 3:6-7 (KJV) In all thy ways acknowledge him, and he shall direct thy paths. ⁷ Be not wise in thine own eyes: fear the LORD, and depart from evil.
Proverbs 3:8 (KJV) It shall be health to thy navel, and marrow to thy bones.
Proverbs 4:20-21 (KJV) My son, attend to my words; incline thine ear unto my sayings. ²¹ Let them not depart from thine eyes; keep them in the midst of thine heart.
Proverbs 4:22 (KJV) For they *are* life unto those that find them, and health to all their flesh.
Proverbs 12:16-18 (KJV) A fool's wrath is presently known: but a prudent *man* covereth shame. ¹⁷ *He that* speaketh truth sheweth forth righteousness: but a false witness deceit. ¹⁸ There is that speaketh like the piercings of a sword: but the tongue of the wise *is* health.
Jeremiah 30:15-17 (KJV) Why criest thou for thine affliction? thy sorrow *is* incurable

for the multitude of thine iniquity: *because* thy sins were increased, I have done these things unto thee. [16] Therefore all they that devour thee shall be devoured; and all thine adversaries, every one of them, shall go into captivity; and they that spoil thee shall be a spoil, and all that prey upon thee will I give for a prey. [17] For I will restore health unto thee, and I will heal thee of thy wounds, saith the LORD; because they called thee an Outcast, *saying*, This *is* Zion, whom no man seeketh after.

Jeremiah 33:6 (KJV) Behold, I will bring it health and cure, and I will cure them, and will reveal unto them the abundance of peace and truth.

3 John 1:1-2 (KJV) The elder unto the well beloved Gaius, whom I love in the truth. [2] Beloved, I wish above all things that thou mayest prosper and be in health, even as thy soul prospereth.

1 Corinthians 12:26-28 (KJV) And whether one member suffer, all the members suffer with it; or one member be honored, all the members rejoice with it. [27] Now ye are the body of Christ, and members in particular. [28] And God hath set some in the church, first apostles, secondarily prophets, thirdly teachers, after

that miracles, then gifts of healings, helps, governments, diversities of tongues.
Exodus 15:26 (KJV) And said, If thou wilt diligently hearken to the voice of the LORD thy God, and wilt do that which is right in his sight, and wilt give ear to his commandments, and keep all his statutes, I will put none of these diseases upon thee, which I have brought upon the Egyptians: for I *am* the LORD that healeth thee.
Psalm 103:1-2 (KJV) Bless the LORD, O my soul: and all that is within me, *bless* his holy name. ² Bless the LORD, O my soul, and forget not all his benefits: ᴾˢ ³ Who forgiveth all thine iniquities; who healeth all thy diseases;
Malachi 4:2 (KJV) But unto you that fear my name shall the Sun of righteousness arise with healing in his wings; and ye shall go forth, and grow up as calves of the stall.
Matthew 4:23 (KJV) And Jesus went about all Galilee, teaching in their synagogues, and preaching the gospel of the kingdom, and healing all manner of sickness and all manner of disease among the people.
Matthew 9:35 (KJV) And Jesus went about all the cities and villages, teaching in their synagogues, and preaching the gospel of the

kingdom, and healing every sickness and every disease among the people.

Luke 9:6 (KJV) And they departed, and went through the towns, preaching the gospel, and healing everywhere.

Acts 10:38 (KJV) How God anointed Jesus of Nazareth with the Holy Ghost and with power: who went about doing good, and healing all that were oppressed of the devil; for God was with him.

1 Corinthians 12:9 (KJV) To another faith by the same Spirit; to another the gifts of healing by the same Spirit;

James 5:14-16 (KJV) Is any sick among you? let him call for the elders of the church; and let them pray over him, anointing him with oil in the name of the Lord:

¹⁵ And the prayer of faith shall save the sick, and the Lord shall raise him up; and if he have committed sins, they shall be forgiven him.

¹⁶ Confess *your* faults one to another, and pray one for another, that ye may be healed. The effectual fervent prayer of a righteous man availeth much.

Luke 5:15 (KJV) But so much the more went there a fame abroad of him: and great multitudes came together to hear, and to be healed by him of their infirmities.

Laughter is good medicine.
A broken spirit dries up the bones.

Norman Cousins lived with severe pain for years. He learned laughter and vitamins helped cure him. Studies were done. It boosts the immune system, reduces pain, stress, relaxes muscles, releases endorphins, eases digestion, balances blood pressure, improves sleep, attitude, and a sense of well-being, precipitating healing. Norman wrote a book in 1979 called "Anatomy of an Illness."

Salvation includes Healing

God has healed humans since the beginning when the right circumstances existed. Since Jesus came, many more have been healed. What changed since the Old Testament?

Jesus' death and resurrection restored the world to the state of sinlessness by shedding His blood to pay for sin, did He not? So why does sin still abound? Did Jesus fail? No, we often fail to take advantage of His sacrifice. Most of the world has ignored His offer of salvation, which also means wholeness.

The same thing applies to sickness and disease. What more could He do than He already did to protect us from sickness? By His stripes we were healed. He is our Great Physician and heals all our diseases. His blood cleanses us from all unrighteousness.

There is nothing more that needs to be done for us to live a life free of sickness – in theory. Do we see this manifesting in our lives? If not, why not? We must learn how to receive it. We have possibly believed some things that were not true for remaining sick, but they do not alter the facts. Jesus took our sicknesses upon Himself. It is sometimes hard to understand that what occurred 2000 years ago heals us now once we grasp it as truth.

John G. Lake, a powerful evangelist, died around 1950. Once he caught the message of healing, amazing miracles occurred. Doctors challenged him to scientifically prove his faith. A man with a broken leg was laid under an x-ray machine. John put his hands on the leg, and while he prayed, the doctors saw the bones knit together! It was physical proof that God, in response to his great faith, healed the man.

Tuberculosis germs were spread on John's hands. While peering into a microscope, doctors watched the germs die on his hands!

In the Old Testament sin often brought sickness, as it does today. The Holy Spirit did not dwell in every believer like He does today. The prophets were endued with power from the Spirit from time to time, and miracles occurred. Elijah raised a boy from the dead using this temporary power. Miriam was healed of leprosy as God used Moses. When Israel sinned, God sent plagues, but then often stopped them by telling the prophets what to do.

James 5 tells us how to be healed when we are sick. There are things we do that open us up to harm.*⁹ Grudge not one against another, brethren, lest ye be condemned: behold, the judge standeth before the door. ¹² But above all things, my brethren, swear not, neither by heaven, neither by the earth, neither by any other oath: but let your yea be yea; and your nay, nay; lest ye fall into condemnation. ¹³ Is any among you afflicted? Let him pray. [14] Is any sick among you? Let him call for the elders of the church; and let them pray over him, anointing him with oil in the name of the Lord: [15] And the prayer of faith shall save the sick, and the Lord shall raise him up; and if he has committed sins, they shall be forgiven him.*

[16] Confess your faults one to another, and pray one for another, that ye may be healed. The effectual fervent prayer of a righteous man availeth much.

**Is God in charge of everything that
happens to us?
Does God's will prevail on the earth?
What DID God promise would happen to
us while we were on the earth?**

I believe: being Omnipotent and all knowing
is not the same as all controlling. We have
free will, and so do those around us. God
knows what will happen because He is not
limited by time, but He does not always
interfere in the affairs of everyone. He does,

however, respond to those who live by faith in His promises, speak it and believe it with all their hearts. A double-minded man receives nothing from God. We must tear down the strongholds in our minds that exalt themselves against the knowledge of God. Jesus asked the paralytic by the pool, "Do you want to be well?" He knew the man's heart.

I believe: the Bible is true. There are things that appear to me to be contradictory sometimes, but the problem is in my lack of wisdom and understanding.

I believe: God has offered his children weapons in which to fight the powers and enemies of God's children. He sent his Holy Spirit to empower believers. Some born-again believers are not equipped to fight as effectively because of unbelief and false teaching about the Holy Spirit.

I believe: only the Bible can be completely trusted. God said we are not to put our trust in man, but in every word that proceeds from the mouth of God. The Word of God must back up all that we are taught. It alone is the truth. All human beings can be deceived. The Holy Spirit will teach us all things.

Jesus said, "I have not come to judge the world but to save it." "Ask anything, believing that you receive it and you shall have it." "Ye Have Not Because Ye Ask Not." James 5:2b

John 10:10 (KJV) The thief cometh not, but for to steal, and to kill, and to destroy: I am come that they might have life, and that they might have *it* more abundantly.

Ephesians 6:11 Put on the full armor of God so you can take your stand against the devil's schemes. For our struggle is not against flesh and blood, but against the rulers, against the authorities, against the powers of this dark world and against the spiritual forces of evil in the heavenly realms. Therefore put on the full armor of God, so that when the day of evil comes, you may be able to stand your ground, and after you have done everything, to stand.

Faith and Doubt

My friend Charlotte is studying with a group that has found many "failed requests" you might say, are due to repressed events in a person's life that must come to the surface before healing can be received. The Holy Spirit during intercession reveals these things so the person can be set free.

When the disciples prayed and sometimes when Jesus prayed, they made sure there were no unbelievers present. No doubters.

Persistent widow. Luke 18. Luke 11:9.
Spirit of infirmity. Luke 13
Unforgiveness, sectarianism. Luke 9:49
Luke 6:27.
Desperation. Issue of blood-touched His garment.
Widow of Nain-she did not ask Jesus, but He came and raised her son from the dead.
Luke 6:11
Is Jesus willing? Luke 5:12
Luke 4:38. Fever rebuked.

There are some who had asked for the Baptism of the Holy Ghost. Since nothing happened right away they decided if Jesus would not give Him to them-the leaders of the church- He does not do this anymore. They turned and decided the belief was a cult notion.

The enemy is blinding them from seeing something so special. God knows we will need this, just like the disciples of old did. It was the plan for the church from the beginning.

Gal.1: 4 Some people are throwing you into confusion and are trying to pervert the gospel of Christ. But even if we or an angel from heaven should preach a gospel other than the one we preached to you, let him be eternally condemned. Who has bewitched you? ...Did you receive the Spirit by observing the law, or by believing what you heard? Are you so foolish? After beginning with the Spirit, are you now trying to attain your goal by human effort? Have you suffered so much for nothing? Does God give you his Spirit and work miracles among you because you observe the law, or because you believe what you heard? Consider Abraham: He believed God, and it was credited to him as righteousness.

The righteous will live by faith. ... By faith we might receive the promise of the Spirit.
2 Tim. 2:3 Endure hardships with us like a good soldier of Christ Jesus.
2 Tim 2:9 I am suffering even to the point of being chained like a criminal. But God's word is not chained. Therefore I endure everything for the sake of the elect, that they too may obtain the salvation in Christ. If we endure, we will reign with Him. If we disown him, he will also disown us. There

will be terrible times in the last days. People will be lovers of themselves, lovers of money, boastful, proud, abusive, disobedient to parents, ungrateful, unholy, without love, unforgiving, slanderous, without self-control, brutal, not lovers of the good, lovers of pleasure rather than God, having a form of godliness but denying its power.

2 Tim. 4:18 The Lord will rescue me from every attack and will bring me safely to his heavenly kingdom. To Him be glory forever and ever. Amen!

Time and time again in the scriptures, we are admonished to ask for those things we need. Ask and it shall be given you, Seek and ye shall find, Knock and it shall be opened unto you. For everyone that asketh receiveth: And he that seeketh findeth; And to him that knocketh it shall be opened. (Matthew 7:7-8)

Why not ask?

Pride--We are too proud to ask. We think we are too strong to humble ourselves enough to ask. We can give, but it is hard to receive. "Better it is to be of an humble spirit with the lowly than to divide the spoil with the PROUD." (Proverbs 16:19)

Unbelief--We don't really believe that God will answer our prayers. He is too busy to hear our prayers. We are not worthy enough to receive. "As thou hast believed, so be it done unto thee." (Matthew 8:13)

Fear--We see God as unapproachable, as an Awesome Creator, a fearsome judge, not as a Father. "If ye then, being evil, know how to give good gifts unto your children, how much more shall your Father, which is in heaven, give good things to them that ask him?" (Matthew 7:11)

How to Receive the Baptism
in the Holy Spirit

Why do we need this experience?

It was God's plan from the beginning. God wants us to have power over the power of the enemy. He wants us to live like Jesus lived. He offers us love, power and a sound mind. He said the Holy Spirit will teach you all things. He wants you to have gifts for the body of Christ and your own family. It brings us into a deeper walk with Him we cannot have without this experience.

Study it in the Word of God

Acts 2:38. Repent and be baptized. Then you shall receive the Holy Ghost if you ask.

Repent means to change, turn from sin, ask forgiveness.

Get immersed in water. Luke 11:9, 10, 13

Use your voice. Be prepared to speak. Expect it to happen. A double-minded man receives nothing from God. Once you are wholly convinced, you will, if you yield your voice.

Expect power from God. Luke 24:39; Acts 1:8; Romans 5:5

Live a good Christian life. Imitate Jesus Christ. Gal. 5:22-25; romans 12L9-21

Use your tongue to talk alone with God. Why? I Cor 14:2, 4

Tell others how easy. Mark 16:15-20

Other gifts that result after this baptism. I Cor 1-17; I Cor 12:16; Ephesians 1:3; 2 Peter 1:3

Faith- one of the nine gifts.

Nine gifts of the Spirit: 1 Cor 12

Healing, miracles, discerning of spirits, tongues, interpretation of tongues, prophecy, word of wisdom, word of knowledge, faith.

Faith is also a fruit of the spirit. Gal 5:22 But the fruit of the spirit is love, joy, peace, long-suffering, gentleness, goodness, faith, meekness, temperance...

Faith is defined as (Heb. 11:1) the substance of things hoped for, and the evidence of things unseen.

Faith is based on knowledge? Do you agree?

Verses about faith. Luke 7:9 Centurion's servant sick-Jesus had not seen such faith in all of Israel. What did he believe?

Luke 7:50 At Simon's house a woman washed his feet with tears (he also said ointment, oil) and kissed them. (Kiss my feet!) Her faith saved her.

Luke 8:2 Mary Magdalene was healed of evil spirits and infirmities.

Luke 17:19 Ten lepers asked for healing. One returned to thank Jesus. He said your faith made you whole.

Luke 18:42 Blind man called to him. What do you want me to do to you? Lord, that I may receive my sight! Receive your sight. Your faith has saved you.

Is faith an important gift from God? Why?

Salvation is a leap of faith. John 3:16

2 Tim 3:15 …scriptures make us wise unto salvation through faith which is in Jesus.

I Peter 1:3-5 you who are kept by God's power thru faith unto salvation. You rejoice though for a season in heaviness through many temptations…that the trial of your faith is tried with fire…you have not seen Him but you love Him, believing, you rejoice!

Salvation means wholeness-in every area, body, mind soul and spirit.

Heb 10:38 justified by faith. We are justified by our faith. Gal 3:24

We receive the promise of the spirit by faith. Gal 3:14, 22

We continue with God by faith. Col. 1:23

Other purposes for faith….

Read Gal 3:11. What does this mean? The just shall live by faith. Rom 1:17

What famous Catholic priest said that?

Must we have faith in someone or something, a focus? Who or what are you trusting most in?

(Money, car, girlfriend, pastor, God, Bible, family)

Rom 3:23 All have sinned, come short of glory… 27, 28 the law of faith justifies us…

Rom 5:1 being justified by faith we have peace with God through our Lord Jesus…

How can we get more faith if we need it and know we don't have enough?

Rom 10:17 hearing and hearing

Does faith originate from us? Can we muster it up?

We cannot be saved unless the Holy Spirit reveals our need to us.

Heb 12:2 Who is the author of our faith? Jesus

James 1:3 The trying of our faith is supposed to do what?

James 1:6 We ask in faith without doubting. We must resist all doubts as lies from the evil one.

What is the evidence of faith? Works. James 2:14 Sit on a chair!

Is the work of faith to believe?

James 2:18 A man says you have faith. I have works. Show me your faith without your works and I will show you my faith by my works. 20 without works is dead. 26 as body without spirit is dead, so faith without works is dead.

What is a prayer of faith? James 5:15 prayer of faith shall save sick, and Lord shall raise him up. If committed sins, shall be forgiven him.

Warning in last days. I Tim 4:1 Now the Spirit speaks expressly, that in the latter times some shall depart from the faith, giving heed to seducing spirits, and doctrines of devils; speaking lies in hypocrisy; having their conscience seared with a hot iron...forbidding to marry, commanding to abstain from meats, which God has created to be received with thanksgiving of them which believe and know the truth.

Remember: falsehood sounds so spiritual! Christianity is a relationship with our creator Father God.

More thoughts about the Gifts of the Spirit

I Cor 12 Nine supernatural gifts, available to all as God decides

Five- fold ministry –teach, preach, evangelist, prophet, apostle

Romans 12:6-serving, teaching, exhorting, mercy, love hospitality

Gift of Holy Spirit-present at new birth and water baptism, endued with power at spiritual baptism done by Jesus if we ask.

God says to desire His gifts.

Why must we know what the Bible says? In the last days many will fall away and be deceived. Bankers do not study counterfeit money. They study real money and the counterfeit is easily spotted. We study the real thing and we will recognize the angel of light when he shows up.

How do you know a true Christian? You will know them by their selfless agape love - all the nine fruits of the spirit. Love is the only one that Satan cannot counterfeit. The real gifts always edify, build up, encourage and help us.

How Satan counterfeits God's wonderful gifts:

1. Prophecy is from God. The counterfeit is called precognition in Satan's kingdom

2. Prayer is real. Mental telepathy is not real prayer.

3. Biblical revelation, words of knowledge and wisdom are Christian terms. Counterfeits are called clairvoyance in the enemy camp.

4. Divine healing from God is counterfeited by Satan, and is called psychic healing. Yes, it does occur, but the end result is not good.

Satan has always tried to prove God was a liar. He told Eve God didn't really say she would die. True, she didn't right then, but she did die. Her spirit went dormant then, and she could no longer commune with God.

Be careful not to give the devil any rights to you in any way. Do not keep any charms, amulets, statues, good luck pieces, Buddhas, bad books...you know what is good and bad. Lots out there these days I never even heard of. When you ask Jesus to baptize you in His Spirit, it is important to first get rid of all such items. They give the enemy legal rights to prevent you from receiving God's best. God said to confess our faults to one another that we may be healed. This is very important. Salvation is free, but some things we want from God require cooperation and some are even conditional.

What did Jesus say?

When Jesus was asked by the disciples to teach them to pray, he began to pray the all-familiar Lord's Prayer. (Matthew 6:11)

In the prayer, we are to ask for four things: Give us this day our daily bread, Forgive us our debts, Lead us not into temptation, Deliver us from evil.

If we asked each day for these four things that would cover our physical needs, our spiritual needs, our protection and our financial needs. That should cover all our needs: our daily walk on this earth and our relationships with others as well as attacks from evil spirits.

Influence of the Neo-Pentecostal/Charismatic movement on Lutheranism

Episcopal priest Dennis Bennett (1917-1991) had perhaps the greatest influence in the charismatic renewal movement within mainline denominations after his announcement that he had received the gift of tongues led to controversy and his resignation. The bishop in Seattle offered him St. Luke's parish that had been scheduled to be closed, and under Bennett's leadership it became a major renewal center for clergy who were hungry for an experience of God. Early figures such as evangelist

Herbert Mjorud of the American Lutheran Church (ALC), journeyed there and were baptized in the Holy Spirit. Mjorud's six-year term with the ALC was not renewed due to controversy over his inclusion of charismatic teaching in his evangelistic work.[9] He traveled the world with a healing ministry and wrote three books, including *Fighting Cancer with Christ*, after receiving healing from lymphatic cancer.[10] This pattern of hearing of the new spiritual experience, praying for and receiving it, and the resulting controversy was repeated in the lives of the many clergy in mainline denominations who were told, "Bloom where you are planted."

Found in:www. holytrinitynewrochelle.org

I must tell you!
God is so good to me!

He found my contact lens in a crack in a wall.
Showed my son Rob my diamond in a pile of gravel!
Gave me a great family.
Brought me to Israel three times!
God gave me a great husband and wonderful kids and in-laws and grandkids and great grands! And great great!
Healed my back, grew my leg longer!
Healed my broken finger!
Fixed my eye after spilling gas in it.
Gave me an A when I had not had time to study.
Saved me from hitting a truck on ice.
Saved me from rolling off a mountain pulling a houseboat!
Protected me from getting hit on my motorcycle on a bridge when it quit on me!
Healed me of flu when group prayed during a motorcycle trip.
Removed pain instantly from bee stings.
Baptized me with His Spirit!
Saved my family!
Saved three sons lost in underwater cave!

Gives me everything on my lists at garage sales.

Gave me marvelous relationships
Filled niece's teeth with silver crosses!
Healed Rog of Type one diabetes
Healed Rog of bursitis
Healed Rog of psoriasis, healed him of
39 broken blood vessels in his eye
 and gave him 20/20 vision!
Healed him of bacterial endocarditis, and
hip problem in hospital after Sommers
prayed.
Saved Lila's mom just before leaving earth!
Saved my Dad six months before he died!
Put Todd's warts off his feet and in his bed
in the night!
Healed Rodney's eyes when he burned them
with UV light!
Healed Betsey my rat of leg infection
Healed Tom's back before surgery
Healed my ingrown toenail when I praised
Him as He told me to-three days of pain.Ten
minutes of obedience!
Jewish patient of mine, accepted Jesus and
died thirty minutes later!
Rog's brother Ron died and came back!
Harold Moore died and returned to tell us
about heaven!

Many miracles with boat accident on highway.
Dog Brandy's leg healed
Friend Sadie's foot healed
Tom's broke ankle slipping on a rock. God healed it!
My friend Yah's baby was born dead and came back to life after binding death and loosing life!
So many more but these just come to mind!

A Fiery Exit

Have you ever seen a house collapse flat to the ground right before your eyes? That is what the neighbors saw when Ollie's house blew up. He was shot right through the wall of the house, between the studs, taking the chunks of plaster lathe right out with him! All they could see was a fireball flying onto the lawn. Ollie was on fire from head to toe.

What happens to skin when polyester pants light up is not a pretty sight. The fibers weave themselves into the body like glue. But God was with Ollie, putting up one barrier after another to protect him. He flew out of the wall, left with only his belt, pants pockets and jacket. The pants had completely dissolved before they could embed into his legs.

In this most astounding intervention, God orchestrated the whole rescue from start to finish. Now you might say, "Why did God let it happen in the first place?" He does not interrupt every tragedy the world gets itself into, but for His children, He moves even the stars in the heavens if necessary. God loves us more than we will ever imagine. He does not want us in pain. If He did, He never would have sent Jesus to die on a cross to give us an escape from hell.

Ollie trusted Jesus so long now he can't remember when he didn't. Some say you must know the date you were born again, but many are saved as little children before they scarcely even need forgiveness. God protected him from death all his life, and he made it triumphantly seventy-seven years so far. He doesn't know of a day that God's Spirit has not been actively walking with him.

Several years ago, Ollie decided to put city water in his house and connect to a city sewer, which required digging a trench in his front yard. Ray, his plumber, hired a man to dig the trench, but no one noticed the backhoe operator was drunk. Circumstances came together to create a disaster. A nearby factory had shut down, but the gas lines that supplied it were still under pressure, and led also to Ollie's property.

The inebriated driver didn't notice the small warning flags posted on the ground to keep this very thing from happening. As he dug the trench he accidentally hooked and pulled up the gas-filled line. Ollie had just entered the basement to turn off his own line at the very moment an enormous supply of gas gushed into his furnace. The furnace instantly exploded, lighting him on fire as a huge fireball worked its way up the stairwell, shooting the human cannonball right through the plaster and out of the house, shattering the cedar siding as he slammed into it.

Ollie felt time slow down, and watched in fascination as each event played out in front of him. He was just a passive participant at this point, and did nothing but stare as he watched flames flow over him. His nylon jacket melted to his body, the cotton lining insulating him from the fire. The only parts of him on fire were his legs, face and hands. Thirty-two percent of his body received third-degree burns, meaning all the skin was burned off, as well as damaging and destroying tender nerve endings.

Meanwhile, his wife and daughter were still in the house, which rose up as the entire house flew off the foundation. An upright grand piano was covered with Ollie's bowling trophies, and a marble trophy soared into Beatrice's head, requiring stitches. She could easily have been killed as those trophies flew around the room, but God had His angels at work. One might say, "Why did she get hurt at all?" If she had not been hit, she and her child would have reached the front door and been crushed to death as the house came down and landed in the basement. Instead, they walked out through the hole made by Ollie's fiery body just as the house collapsed behind them. It was all over in seven minutes!

Ollie's story is amazing. Not a bone was broken during his flight from the basement. His glasses remained on! His recovery in the burns center at Bronson hospital was remarkable. The process of removing dead tissue after severe burns is terribly painful, but not once did he even cry out, which if you have ever gone through such a thing, you understand this is nearly impossible, except for God's grace and mercy. He knows the profound power of rejoicing in his tribulations. **John 16:33 (KJV)** *These things I have spoken unto you, that in me ye might have peace. In the world ye shall have tribulation: but be of good cheer; I have overcome the world.*

He listens to God. At the hospital he was told it would likely take about six months before he could leave the hospital. He denied it, saying he would be home by his daughter's birthday. It was fifteen days away, and he made it! **Psalm 91:2 (KJV***) I will say of the LORD, He is my refuge and my fortress: my God; in him will I trust.*

The doctor expected Ollie to get aspiration pneumonia from breathing in while on fire, but he never got it. He was also prepared to graft skin, but God grew all new skin without the need for any grafts, and he has not one scar on his entire body!

Ollie had many other scrapes with death, but **Romans 8:37 (KJV)** says, *Nay, in all these things we are more than conquerors through him that loved us.* He had a heart valve that was nearly non-functioning, and some veins and arteries 95% closed up. When the doctor opened him up and replaced the valve with a pig valve, he found two of the blocked vessels had already built up back-up pathways to supply his heart, so he only had two vessels replaced. The doctor said he heals faster than a teenager.

His wife passed away only four months ago, but he is still strong in his faith, spreading the gospel every way he can. I am so proud to call Ollie my friend.

John 8:51 (KJV) *Verily, verily, I say unto you, If a man keep my saying, he shall never see death.*

Prisoners of Hope

Do you feel like a prisoner? There are those imprisoned by bars around them. This is the picture we have of a prisoner. Some are held captive by habits they feel they cannot change, authorities above them that control every move they make, and some are bound by inabilities to move about freely for various reasons. My friend Linda had a serious infection at age sixteen that paralyzed her from the neck down. She was surely a prisoner of those who cared for her.

Paul weighed seven hundred pounds. The dear man didn't ask for a faulty metabolism. He was held down by his enormous weight and frequent discouragement over his imprisonment. He died at thirty-seven, and then learned what the freedom he hoped for was all about.

My brother-in-law considered me quite strange for many years because I believed in God as my hope of eternal life. One day I was reading a great book called, "Life after Life." I felt an urgent desire to call him. He was recovering from a heart bypass operation. As we talked, I asked him what happened during surgery, not knowing something really did! He got all choked up, and suddenly I knew he had died! I said, "You died, didn't you?" He hesitated, and then choked out the word, "Yes!" Then he spoke in a whisper, "I could see everything, and I was floating on the ceiling looking down at the doctors and at my body! I was so free! It was such a wonderful peace! I was so angry to find myself being sucked back into my body! But I will never look at life the same way again!" He never mocked me after that, and his life greatly changed for the better. He has no fear of death.

You and I are prisoners of gravity, of the rules of culture, of a need to sleep and eat and everything that encumbers us in these physical bodies. One day we will have bodies that are unbound by such things. We will never die, we will not be bound by gravity, or worries and fears and habits, and we will then realize that we spent our lives on earth as "Prisoners of Hope." "Without a vision, my people perish."

There are those that believe this is not true, and to put such thoughts into a person's mind is wrong and unfair. I strongly disagree. Without hope of something wonderful in our future, life is not sufficient in and of itself. I used to say if what I believe about eternity turns out to be false, I have lost nothing. The joy of expectation is so delightful that it does me no harm to believe it is true. But I now believe it with all my heart. I understand now how the martyrs that died for their faith were able to sing even while they were burned alive at the stake. They were prisoners of supernatural hope and faith. They were about to experience what until then had been a great expectation. Our precious God has given us free will so we are not really prisoners at all. Jesus came to set us free!

Had to be an Angel

My husband Rog was in the hospital. His nurse promised me that I could sit with him during the night after he had open heart surgery. After he was settled in his room, the shift changed, and the new nurse refused to let me in! I had to go out in the waiting room and curl up on a sofa for the night.

The next morning I was allowed in the room, and he told me an amazing story. "I came out of surgery with a ventilator stuck in my mouth, the kind you only have while you are anesthetized. It went all the way down my throat. My hands were held down and I couldn't call for help. I panicked.

Sweat was rolling down my face from stark terror. I felt so helpless!"

He said a tall black man dressed all in white suddenly showed up and looking at his face, spoke calmly and started bathing him. As he bathed and talked, Rog relaxed and eventually fell asleep. Later when the nurse took out the vent, Rog told her about the wonderful black man that helped keep him sane. The nurse insisted that no one could have come in there, and there was no black man working in that department. "It is impossible that such a person could have been in your room, Mr. Parrott!"

I am now convinced God sent an angel when he was desperate.

I Want to be Free
By Jennifer

How far down must a person fall before he sees the truth? I fell nearly into hell before I was rescued. I spent thirteen years of my life where I was merely escaping the inevitable, thirteen years without God. I was left with a crying mother and a heart full of unbearable demons. Who would have known God could pour such great miracles into such a life, while every day I lived in fear, believing forgiveness and acceptance was impossible. One question tormented me. Why was it so easy to believe in the devil, yet so hard to believe in God?

I remember growing up as a kid; my

grandma was very religious and I attended her church with my friends. I was never forced to go. I didn't really understand much of it, but I always had fun. Then I became a teenager.

There is always that one crowd that doesn't make right choices. I was one of those people who felt like they really didn't fit in. I saw the kids around me in school as sociable, easily liked, and I would even say normal or average. I had no idea it was normal to feel like a misfit as a teenager. We will avoid the pain of rejection at all cost. We want to fit in, but we don't know what extremes are required from that particular group and at what point we need to stop or bail out. I just wanted to belong.

Not yet mature enough to make wise choices, I ended up choosing the wrong friends. As a result I did a lot of things I regret. It is said that you become like those you hang out with; birds of a feather flock together; and my choice of friends forever changed my life.

Exposure to what they liked changed my taste in music to hardcore rock with screaming and rage, which influenced a change in my appearance. I started to dress with all black clothing and tricked-out hair. I started to drift into the 'Satanist' stuff, because somewhere in my mind it made sense, but it sucked me down a path toward death. First came depression, then self-mutilation and finally thoughts of suicide. My life spiraled downward and soon I just wanted my life to end. I lost the nice friends I did have, confused my family, and even more important, I lost a part of myself.

Mutilating one's self has confused the experts for ages. It used to be considered a failed suicide attempt, but that is not it. People with addictions are similar in the sense they have somehow lost control of what they do to themselves. Some other power takes them over. It is the same once a person starts cutting himself. It seems to give a feeling of relief, even though it is shocking to feel the pain and see your blood pour out of your body. What does a person gain by such an action? It was simply a step into the occult world brought about by crazy music and irrational thought patterns where there were no boundaries.

I can remember every detail of the day I first tried it. With a rusty old carpenter knife, I slit my arm open, and by the time I was done, I had more than sixty cuts scattered all along my body. I remember the look on my mom's face! She walked into my room and found me holding a bloody towel with a knife to my wrist. I knew what I was doing was destructive and wrong and didn't understand what made me even do such a thing. I wanted to die of shame. I felt like the most worthless person and a huge disappointment to my family. Suicide seemed like my only option. If I could have sunk through the floor, I would have.

This awful obsession continued in secret, and made me very weak, emotionally, mentally, and physically. One day I simply fell apart, crying and trembling, too weak even to walk. My mom was exhausted, having tried everything she knew, at her wits' end, with no idea how to stop me from self-destruction.

I made the choice to admit myself into a hospital with some hope that I'd get well. I remember my mom bringing me a Bible. With not much else to do there, terribly confused and hopeless, I decided to read my new Bible and pray. I was eventually released from the hospital and had gained a bit of faith and hope, but not enough to solve my problems, still struggling with depression.

During this process of change, my mom introduced me to her friend Janie, who took me to church with her, but the problem continued; I was still not free, and my faith in God was still zero to none. The pastor's words made no sense and the thought of God's love and forgiveness was just a lie to me.

Janie became a guardian to me, like the light at the end of a tunnel. She kept bringing me to her church where I met A LOT of really nice people. I didn't really believe anything the pastor preached. I was just stubborn and didn't want to accept the facts about Jesus, and that someone actually cared.

Once again, I was admitted into another hospital, but this time I was starting to gain a new perspective. I remember how everyone there thought I was crazy because I would sit there by myself in a corner, look up at the sky and just cry and scream to God. In my room I would sing and pray to him on my knees just asking, "Why?" I finally just surrendered. I got on my knees in my room and said, "God, I have no direction other than you to help me through this all. I just need your hand in guidance to lead my way." This time I kept my head focused on getting better. I prayed desperate prayers every single night I was there.

That day, I could tell everything in me had changed. I was discharged from the hospital with a completely new perspective and with God as my Lord and Savior. I went to my church and confessed my faith in Jesus Christ and was saved. I realized Jesus paid for my sins and wrong ways. I feel accepted and not so alone. I started to see my life turn around as God began having his way with me.

Today, I see everything different. I no longer turn to cutting to solve my problems. My music has turned to worship and my clothes are full of color. God is now the one I turn to whenever any problem arises. He continues to make changes in my life every day and is guiding me on my path to change the world around me. That decision to be saved was the best one I could ever make because only God can turn lives into miracles. I will never forget what he has done for me. I've been attending church and I try to help them out whenever I can. They showed me Jesus and gave me hope. I am ready for whatever life has in store for me, and I feel like I can take on the world. "Life is meant to be lived in one direction-upward." God CHANGED my life.

The hospital contained me and protected me for a time, but only God set me free, using these scriptures.

Psalm 6:1-10 (KJV)
O LORD, rebuke me not in thine anger, neither chasten me in thy hot displeasure. [2] Have mercy upon me, O LORD; for I *am* weak: O LORD, heal me; for my bones are vexed. [3] My soul is also sore vexed: but thou, O LORD, how long? [4] Return, O LORD, deliver my soul: oh save me for thy mercies' sake. [5] For in death *there is* no remembrance of thee: in the grave who shall give thee thanks? [6] I am weary with my groaning; all the night

make I my bed to swim; I water my couch with my tears. [7] Mine eye is consumed because of grief; it waxeth old because of all mine enemies. [8] Depart from me, all ye workers of iniquity; for the LORD hath heard the voice of my weeping. [9] The LORD hath heard my supplication; the LORD will receive my prayer. [10] Let all mine enemies be ashamed and sore vexed: let them return *and* be ashamed suddenly.

Kingdom of the Cults

When we married, my father-in-law was a Freemason. My mother-in-law was in the Eastern Star. My husband became a Freemason and later what was called the "Worshipful Master". For twenty years our activities centered on Masonry and the Shrine. There was a lot of drinking and partying in the Shrine, but not so much with the Masons.

Roger renounced Masonry a few years ago when he was afraid of dying from a heart problem he had. Friends shared an audiotape with him and he realized he had been deceived, having considered Freemasonry simply a brotherhood organization. He sensed his physical problems might have connections with his mistaken devotion to the wrong god. He repented of his involvement and renounced Masonry that night. The next day he had open-heart surgery with two bypasses and a new valve, and had absolutely no pain during several weeks of recovery, which was a great miracle. Others in the waiting rooms with him had no such a blessing after their similar surgery!

Our friend Bob spent many years in Mormonism. When he learned the deception in Mormonism and the ties to Masonry, (the founder of Mormonism, Joseph Smith and his brother Hyrum, were also Masons.) Bob began to study over a thousand books on both religions (yes, Masonry IS a religion), including cryptic books for Masons only. He now speaks all over the country, mostly in churches. One day he went to a funeral and the hair on his neck stood up. He turned to see a group of men marching in with aprons on, wearing white gloves, chanting and breaking leaves over the coffin. His Masonic father said he wanted a funeral like that. "Over my dead body!" our friend said.

His father later renounced Masonry and died a Christian, devoted only to Jesus Christ.

Masonry began benignly with the stonemasons in Solomon's time. They learned secret handshakes and signs to show other masons they belonged to the craft of stonemasonry, but nothing more. Spiritual Masonry began much later. The first Grand lodge met in England in 1717. Masonry was involved in the French and American Revolutions, and a conspiratorial part of America's history. Many in the first Congress were Masons. The Declaration of Independence was written on a Masonic white lambskin apron. Masons designed the Congressional Medal of Honor, which has on it a pentagram, the most powerful satanic emblem.

The statue of Liberty was a gift from Masons in France to the American Masons. It is filled with occult symbols.

Initiates are told this is a brotherhood organization that allows all religions to join, and that it is not a religion, but it definitely is. It is not Christian, by any means. The secret identity of God is Jabulon, and stands for Jehovah, Ba'al, and Osiris, the Egyptian sun god. The swearing-in ceremony and the rituals make this a religion in honor of demons. The key demon is the Goat of Mendes or Baphomet.

When a Mason receives his apron, he is told it should be his covering when they stand before the great white throne judgment of God. They don't realize this is the judgment of the damned!

The 'sacred' word learned at a certain level of the Scottish rite is Abbadon. This is the angel of the bottomless pit. Rev.9:11

Blue Lodge members are sworn to keep brethren's secrets, murder and treason excepted. Royal Arch Masons are sworn to protect even murder and treason. Imagine going to a court of law and expecting a fair trial when the judge is upholding first his oath to the Masons. If you hear of a crazy court case that is not going fairly, you might examine the roots of Masonry.

Scriptures and Bible teachings are sometimes quoted in Masonry but the name of Jesus Christ is generally omitted.

Those that partake of only the first thirty-two degrees of Masonry, though they have made terrible vows, have not taken communion of the dead, drinking wine from a human skull, as in the higher levels of the Scottish rite, I believe it was the 33rd degree.

Once they study and pass the 32nd degree, they may go into the Shrine-for a price, of course. Their vows include an oath that says, "May Allah, the god of Arab, Moslem, and Mohammedan, the god of our fathers, support me..." Allah is not God the Father of Jesus Christ! It is a deity entombed in a building in Mecca where Islam worships it. No Christian can submit to or swear allegiance to this other god, Allah.

Why is the Fez they wear red? The Muslims butchered forty-five thousand people in the city of Fez that refused to bow to Allah. They dipped their white hats in the blood of the Christian martyrs.

The Orlando Sentinel published a report about the percentage of the money collected by Shriners went to the Shrine hospitals. You may check for yourself.

If families of Masons are having sickness or any other cursed things bothering them, they need to examine their relationship with God. He is a jealous God, and has a right to be. He gave His only Son to save us. Nobody else deserves our allegiance. Masonry brings a curse into families to the third and fourth generation of those that have turned from God. God honors repentance from the heart and forgives sin.

There are many Masons sitting in churches unaware that they have been disloyal to God. They simply have been deceived. It does not help to condemn them, but pray and share what you know to be true if they will listen. Many great articles are found on the Internet. The above information came from one called, "Freemasonry and the Church" by Ed Decker. Type in 'Christians and Freemasonry.' Used with permission.

Healing Scriptures
FOR THOSE WHO LOVE TO STUDY
GOD'S WORD

Gen 1:26-30

Gen 2:17 But of the tree of the knowledge of good and evil, thou shalt not eat of it: for in the day that thou eatest thereof thou shalt surely die.

Rom. 5:12-21 Therefore, just as through one man sin entered the world, and death through sin, and thus death spread to all men, because all sinned.[13] (For until the law sin was in the world, but sin is not imputed when there is no law. [14] Nevertheless death reigned from Adam to Moses, even over those who had not sinned according to the likeness of the transgression of Adam, who is a type of Him who was to come.

[15] But the free gift *is* not like the offense. For if by the one man's offense many died, much more the grace of God and the gift by the grace of the one Man, Jesus Christ, abounded to many. [16] And the gift *is* not like *that which came* through the one who sinned. For the judgment *which came* from one *offense resulted* in condemnation, but the free gift *which came* from many offenses *resulted* in justification. [17] For if by the one man's offense death reigned through the one, much more those who receive abundance of grace and of the gift of righteousness will reign in life through the One, Jesus Christ.) [18] Therefore, as through one man's offense *judgment* came to all men, resulting in condemnation, even so through one Man's righteous act *the free gift came* to all men, resulting in justification of life. [19] For as by one man's disobedience many were made sinners, so also by one Man's obedience many will be made righteous. [20] Moreover the law entered that the offense might abound. But where sin abounded, grace abounded much more, [21] so that as sin reigned in death, even so grace might reign through righteousness to eternal life through Jesus Christ our Lord.

Gen 3:15 And I will put enmity Between you and the woman, And between your seed and her Seed; He shall bruise your head, And you shall bruise His heel."

Gen. 20:1-18
And Abraham journeyed from there to the South, and dwelt between Kadesh and Shur, and stayed in Gerar. ² Now Abraham said of Sarah his wife, "She *is* my sister." And Abimelech king of Gerar sent and took Sarah. ³ But God came to Abimelech in a dream by night, and said to him, "Indeed you *are* a dead man because of the woman whom you have taken, for she *is* a man's wife." ⁴ But Abimelech had not come near her; and he said, "Lord, will You slay a righteous nation also? ⁵ Did he not say to me, 'She *is* my sister'? And she, even she herself said, 'He *is* my brother.' In the integrity of my heart and innocence of my hands I have done this." ⁶ And God said to him in a dream, "Yes, I know that you did this in the integrity of your heart. For I also withheld you from sinning against Me; therefore I did not let you touch her. ⁷ Now therefore, restore the man's wife; for he *is* a prophet, and he will pray for you and you shall live. But if you do not restore *her*,

know that you shall surely die, you and all who *are* yours." [8] So Abimelech rose early in the morning, called all his servants, and told all these things in their hearing; and the men were very much afraid. [9] And Abimelech called Abraham and said to him, "What have you done to us? How have I offended you, that you have brought on me and on my kingdom a great sin? You have done deeds to me that ought not to be done." [10] Then Abimelech said to Abraham, "What did you have in view, that you have done this thing?" [11] And Abraham said, "Because I thought, surely the fear of God *is* not in this place; and they will kill me on account of my wife. [12] **But indeed *she is* truly my sister. She *is* the daughter of my father, but not the daughter of my mother**; and she became my wife. [13] And it came to pass, when God caused me to wander from my father's house, that I said to her, 'This *is* your kindness that you should do for me: in every place, wherever we go, say of me, "He *is* my brother."

[14] Then Abimelech took sheep, oxen, and male and female servants, and gave *them* to Abraham; and he restored Sarah his wife to him. [15] And Abimelech said, "See, my land *is*

before you; dwell where it pleases you."
[16] Then to Sarah he said, "Behold, I have given your brother a thousand *pieces* of silver; indeed this vindicates you[4] before all who *are* with you and before everybody." Thus she was rebuked. [17] So Abraham prayed to God; and God healed Abimelech, his wife, and his female servants. Then they bore *children;* [18] for the LORD had closed up all the wombs of the house of Abimelech because of Sarah, Abraham's wife.

Gen. 20:7,17 Now therefore, restore the man's wife; for he *is* a prophet, and he will pray for you and you shall live. But if you do not restore *her,* know that you shall surely die, you and all who *are* yours." So Abraham prayed to God; and God healed Abimelech, his wife, and his female servants. Then they bore *children;*

Ex. 15:26 and said, "If you diligently heed the voice of the LORD your God and do what is right in His sight, give ear to His commandments and keep all His statutes, I will put none of the diseases on you which I have brought on the Egyptians. For I *am* the LORD who heals you."

Ps 103:3 Who forgives all your iniquities, Who heals all your diseases,

Ps 105:7 He *is* the LORD our God; His judgments *are* in all the earth. [8] He remembers His covenant forever, The word *which* He commanded, for a thousand generations,

Mt. 8:17 When evening had come, they brought to Him many who were demon-possessed. And He cast out the spirits with a word, and healed all who were sick, [17] that it might be fulfilled which was spoken by Isaiah the prophet, saying: *"He Himself took our infirmities And bore our sicknesses.* "[7]

John 3:14 And as Moses lifted up the serpent in the wilderness, even so must the Son of Man be lifted up, [15] that whoever believes in Him should not perish but[15]have eternal life.

Lev 26
Dt 28
Ps 91
Is 58

James 5:14-18 Is anyone among you sick? Let him call for the elders of the church, and let them pray over him, anointing him with oil in the name of the Lord. [15] And the prayer of faith will save the sick, and the Lord will raise him up. And if he has committed sins, he will be forgiven. [16] Confess *your* trespasses[5] to one another, and pray for one another, that you may be healed. The effective, fervent prayer of a righteous man avails much. [17] Elijah was a man with a nature like ours, and he prayed earnestly that it would not rain; and it did not rain on the land for three years and six months. [18] And he prayed again, and the heaven gave rain, and the earth produced its fruit.

Job 33:12-30
Ps 38
Ps 103:3
Num 12:13-16; 21:9

I Cor 5:1-5 It is actually reported *that there is* sexual immorality among you, and such sexual immorality as is not even named[1] among the Gentiles--that a man has his father's wife! [2] And you are puffed up, and have not rather mourned, that he who has done this deed might be taken away from among you. ³ For I indeed, as absent in body but present in spirit, have already judged (as though I were present) him who has so done this deed. ⁴ In the name of our Lord Jesus Christ, when you are gathered together, along with my spirit, with the power of our Lord Jesus Christ, ⁵ deliver such a one to Satan for the destruction of the flesh, that his spirit may be saved in the day of the Lord Jesus.[2]

2 Cor 2:6-11⁶ This punishment which *was inflicted* by the majority *is* sufficient for such a man, ⁷ so that, on the contrary, you *ought* rather to forgive and comfort *him,* lest perhaps such a one be swallowed up with too much sorrow. ⁸ Therefore I urge you to reaffirm *your* love to him. ⁹ For to this end I also wrote, that I might put you to the test, whether you are obedient in all things. ¹⁰ Now whom you forgive anything, I also *forgive.* For if indeed I have forgiven anything, I have forgiven[19] that one for your sakes in the presence of Christ, ¹¹ lest Satan should take advantage of us; for we are not ignorant of his devices.

Gal 6:7-8 Do not be deceived, God is not mocked; for whatever a man sows, that he will also reap. [8] For he who sows to his flesh will of the flesh reap corruption, but he who sows to the Spirit will of the Spirit reap everlasting life.

Gen 20:7,17

Job 42:1-12 Then Job answered the LORD and said: [2] "I know that You can do everything, And that no purpose *of Yours* can be withheld from You. [3] *You asked,* 'Who *is* this who hides counsel without knowledge?' Therefore I have uttered what I did not understand, Things too wonderful for me, which I did not know. [4] Listen, please, and let me speak; *You said,* 'I will question you, and you shall answer Me.' [5] "I have heard of You by the hearing of the ear, But now my eye sees You. [6] Therefore I abhor *myself,* And repent in dust and ashes." [7] And so it was, after the LORD had spoken these words to Job, that the LORD said to Eliphaz the Temanite, "My wrath is aroused against you and your two friends, for you have not spoken of Me *what is* right, as My servant Job *has.*

[8] Now therefore, take for yourselves seven bulls and seven rams, go to My servant Job, and offer up for yourselves a burnt offering; and My servant Job shall pray for you. For I will accept him, lest I deal with you *according to your* folly; because you have not spoken of Me *what is* right, as My servant Job *has."* [9] So Eliphaz the Temanite and Bildad the Shuhite *and* Zophar the Naamathite went and did as the LORD commanded them; for the LORD had accepted Job. [10] And the LORD restored Job's losses[5] when he prayed for his friends. Indeed the LORD gave Job twice as much as he had before. [11] Then all his brothers, all his sisters, and all those who had been his acquaintances before, came to him and ate food with him in his house; and they consoled him and comforted him for all the adversity that the LORD had brought upon him. Each one gave him a piece of silver and each a ring of gold. [12] Now the LORD blessed the latter *days* of Job more than his beginning; for he had fourteen thousand sheep, six thousand camels, one thousand yoke of oxen, and one thousand female donkeys.

14. Christ came to redeem from sin and sickness.

Gal 3:1-13

Rom 8:11

Isaiah 35

Isaiah 53

Isaiah 61:1-2

Mk 16:17 And these signs will follow those who believe: In My name they will cast out demons; they will speak with new tongues; [18] they[2]will take up serpents; and if they drink anything deadly, it will by no means hurt them; they will lay hands on the sick, and they will recover."

How to enter the Kingdom of God and become a Christian:

We need to realize we are all sinners. Then:

1. Admit to God you have sinned in your life, like everyone else. Romans 3:23 says, "All have sinned and come short of the glory of God."

2. Believe in your heart that Christ died for your sins and that He rose again the third day from the dead in the flesh. John 3:16 says "God sent his only begotten son, that whoever believes on him shall be saved.

3. Talk to God: It is simple enough for children to understand. We are all children in God's eyes. You can say, Dear Jesus, I choose to believe you became my substitute, died for me and rose again, I call on your name and ask you to save me. Thank you. Amen.

4. Tell someone what you did. Telling a Christian is easiest. Romans 10:9 says, "If you will confess with your mouth that Jesus is Lord, and believe in your heart that God raised him from the dead, you shall be saved."

This is the only way to get to heaven, by believing in Jesus. We do not get there by anything we do. He is like a bridge to the Father.

Welcome to the Family of God! You have become a new creature! Old things have passed away, and all things have become new.

Assurance of Our Salvation

When you prayed for salvation, did it change your life? Did you mean it? Do you still believe it? So what hope do we have that we will make it to heaven when we die?

2 Peter 1:10 says: Therefore, my brothers, be all the more eager to make your calling and election sure. For if you do these things, you will never fall, (NIV)

As we grow and increase our understanding, these changes will begin to occur. If we fall away, God is just to forgive us when we repent, return, change. **1 John 1:9**
Ephesians 2:8 It is by grace you have been saved through faith.
1 John 5:13 (KJV) Determine to obey Jesus and submit to His Lordship in our lives.
1 John 2:3 And hereby we do know that we know him, if we keep his commandments.
John 14:15
1 John 2:15 (KJV) Practice righteousness rather than sin.
1 John 2:29 (NKJV) We have genuine love for God and love for others. Jesus said we fulfill His commands if we love God with a whole heart, and love others as ourselves.

1 John 3:14 (NKJV) We have the awareness of the presence of the Holy Spirit within us.

1 John 3:24 Those who obey God's commandments remain in fellowship with him, and he with them. And we know he lives in us because the Spirit he gave us lives in us. **(NLT)** (*We do not lose our salvation if we fail to do the right things. We may lose fellowship until we turn back to Him.*)

We follow Jesus' example and live as he did.

1 John 2:6 (NKJV) He who says he abides in Him ought himself also to walk just as He walked.

We continue to transform our minds studying in the Bible.

1 John 2:24 (KJV) Let that therefore abide in you, which ye have heard from the beginning. If that which ye have heard from the beginning shall remain in you, ye also shall continue in the Son, and in the Father.

Earnestly hope for the return of Jesus Christ for us.

1 John 3:2-3 (NKJV) Beloved, now are we children of God, and it has not yet been revealed what we shall be: but we know that, when he is revealed, we shall be like him; for we shall see him as he is. [3] And everyone who has this hope in Him purifies himself, just as He is pure.

A healthy conscience will wake you in the night with conviction over sin, and motivate you to confess, repent and to lead you to restoration.

The enemy of your soul will convince you to rationalize away your sin, encourage you to take chemicals, food, or alcohol to numb your conscience, and hold onto the sin. Eventually sin will bring death.

Satan came to steal, kill and destroy. Jesus said, "I have come to bring you life and that more abundantly."

I would love to hear your remarks, good or bad. All of them are valid. My Email is granparrott@gmail.com.

Other books I have written can be found on Amazon and Kindle. You will find several subjects there, addiction recoveries, amazing moments in our lives, dreams and visions, plus many more. Check it out.

Judy Parrott

A Life Worth Living (my autobiography)
Alien and other Mysteries.
Break Every Chain (How to overcome addictions)
Dreams and Visions of the Future.
Evidence of His Presence.
Heart to Heart (like Jesus Calling)
*His Journey to Eternity (*my husband Rog's life story)
Motorcycle Miracles.
Mysterious Wonders.
Quicksand-about addictions.
Shout from the Housetops (like Jesus Calling)
Supernatural Events from God.

Made in the USA
Columbia, SC
09 September 2020